PREFACE

1. Scope

This publication provides doctrine for planning and conducting joint noncombatant evacuation operations throughout the range of military operations. Specific information on repatriation operations is also provided.

2. Purpose

This publication has been prepared under the direction of the Chairman of the Joint Chiefs of Staff. It sets forth joint doctrine to govern the activities and performance of the Armed Forces of the United States in operations and provides the doctrinal basis for interagency coordination and for US military involvement in multinational operations. It provides military guidance for the exercise of authority by combatant commanders and other joint force commanders (JFCs) and prescribes joint doctrine for operations and training. It provides military guidance for use by the Armed Forces in preparing their appropriate plans. It is not the intent of this publication to restrict the authority of the JFC from organizing the force and executing the mission in a manner the JFC deems most appropriate to ensure unity of effort in the accomplishment of the overall objective.

3. Application

a. Joint doctrine established in this publication applies to the commanders of combatant commands, subunified commands, joint task forces, subordinate components of these commands, and the Services.

b. The guidance in this publication is authoritative; as such, this doctrine will be followed except when, in the judgment of the commander, exceptional circumstances dictate otherwise. If conflicts arise between the contents of this publication and the contents of Service publications, this publication will take precedence unless the Chairman of the Joint Chiefs of Staff, normally in coordination with the other members of the Joint Chiefs of Staff, has provided more current and specific guidance. Commanders of forces operating as part of a multinational (alliance or coalition) military command should follow multinational doctrine and procedures ratified by the United States. For doctrine and procedures not ratified by the United States, commanders should evaluate and follow the multinational command's doctrine and procedures, where applicable and consistent with US law, regulations, and doctrine.

For the Chairman of the Joint Chiefs of Staff:

WILLIAM E. GORTNEY
VADM, USN
Director, Joint Staff

Intentionally Blank

SUMMARY OF CHANGES
CHANGE 1 TO JOINT PUBLICATION 3-68
DATED 22 JANUARY 2007

- **Added a vignette on the issue of evacuating third country nationals to Chapter I, "Overview."**

- **Added language per the Department of State policy on the issue of evacuating pets.**

- **Incorporated additional considerations (strategic communication, military deception, defense support to public diplomacy, and information sharing) as part of Chapter V, "Employment and Evacuation Operation Procedures" under paragraph 4, "General Considerations."**

- **Changed "geospatial intelligence contingency packages" to "geospatial intelligence base for contingency operations" per the National Geospatial-Intelligence Agency's change in terminology.**

- **Deleted Appendix C, "Psychological Operations Considerations."**

- **Updated DD Form 2585 in Appendix F, "Repatriation Processing Center Processing Sheet."**

Intentionally Blank

TABLE OF CONTENTS

FIGURE

Intentionally Blank

EXECUTIVE SUMMARY
COMMANDER'S OVERVIEW

- **Provides an Overview of Noncombatant Evacuation Operations (NEOs)**

- **Discusses NEO Roles, Coordination, and Interaction**

- **Covers NEO Command and Control**

- **Discusses Contingency and Predeployment Planning Considerations**

- **Covers Employment and Evacuation Operation Procedures**

- **Provides Guidance on Evacuee Processing**

- **Discusses NEO Intermediate Staging Base and Safe Haven Operations**

Overview

A noncombatant evacuation operation (NEO) is conducted to evacuate US citizens whose lives are in danger.

Noncombatant evacuation operations (NEOs) are conducted to assist the Department of State (DOS) in evacuating US citizens, Department of Defense (DOD) civilian personnel, and designated host nation (HN) and third country nationals (TCNs) whose lives are in danger from locations in a foreign nation to an appropriate safe haven. The United States Government (USG) will consider evacuating TCNs and host country nationals on a case-by-case, space available/reimbursable basis. Although normally considered in connection with hostile action, evacuation may also be conducted in anticipation of, or in response to, any natural or man-made disaster.

NEOs have special characteristics.

NEOs have humanitarian, military, economic, diplomatic, and political implications. NEOs usually involve swift insertion of a force, temporary occupation of an objective, and a planned withdrawal upon completion of the mission.

Special nature of evacuation operations.

The command and control structure and the political and diplomatic factors involved in timing the execution of the military support of NEOs make them different from other military operations. During NEOs, the US ambassador, not the geographic combatant commander (GCC) or subordinate joint force commander (JFC), is the senior USG authority for the evacuation and, as such, is ultimately responsible for the successful completion of the NEO and the safety of the evacuees. The decision to evacuate a US embassy and the order to execute a NEO is political.

The GCC may decide to create a joint task force (JTF) to conduct a NEO or may task a component commander to conduct the NEO.

Rules of engagement may be such that the JTF should be prepared to protect personnel (military and evacuees) from a wide variety of threats while not necessarily having the authority to preempt hostile actions by proactive military measures.

NEOs may occur in permissive, uncertain, or hostile environments.

Evacuation operations are characterized by uncertainty and may be directed without warning because of sudden changes in a country's government, reoriented diplomatic or military relationships with the United States, a sudden hostile threat to US citizens from a force within or external to an HN, or a devastating natural or man-made disaster. Some key factors in noncombatant evacuation planning are situational awareness; a correct appraisal and understanding of the changing diplomatic, political, and military environment in which the evacuation force will operate; time constraints and risk; and preparation of the evacuation force for a situation that may rapidly move from permissive to uncertain or hostile. Alternative plans should be developed for permissive, uncertain, and hostile environments.

Roles Coordination and Interaction

At all levels, Department of Defense and Department of State personnel need to cooperate to successfully execute the NEO.

Washington Liaison Group (WLG). Secretary of State (SECSTATE) and Secretary of Defense (SecDef) established the WLG to ensure coordination of the work of their departments in fulfilling their responsibilities for protection and evacuation of US citizens abroad. The WLG is responsible for coordination and implementation at the national level of all emergency and evacuation plans by DOS and DOD and by other USG agencies as appropriate.

SECSTATE and SecDef have established regional liaison groups (RLGs) colocated with combatant commands as necessary to ensure coordination of emergency and evacuation planning by their departments in the field. Each RLG is chaired by a DOS representative. Membership includes representatives of the appropriate combatant commander and any subordinate component commands as desired.

Emergency Action Committee (EAC). This organization is established at a foreign service post by the ambassador for the purpose of directing and coordinating the post's response to contingencies as well as drafting the post's emergency action plan (EAP). The EAC is the focal point for DOS and DOD evacuation site interface.

United States embassy representatives.

The ambassador is the personal representative of the President to the government of the foreign country or to the intergovernmental organization (IGO) to which he or she is accredited and, as such, is the chief of mission (COM), responsible for recommending and implementing national policy regarding the foreign country or IGO and for overseeing the activities of USG employees in the mission. The ambassador has extraordinary decision-making authority as the senior USG official on the ground during crises.

United States Defense Attaché Office is an office of Service attachés managed by the Defense Intelligence Agency. A US senior defense official/defense attaché (SDO/DATT) heads the defense attaché office in country and is a member of the country team. The SDO/DATT is the COM's principal military advisor on defense and national security issues, the senior diplomatically accredited DOD military officer assigned to a US diplomatic mission, and the single point of contact for all DOD matters involving the embassy or DOD elements assigned to or working from the embassy.

The **Security Assistance Officer (SAO)** maintains liaison with the HN military forces and is authorized by law to perform certain military functions with the HN military. The advance party forward command element (FCE) should coordinate with the SAO.

Secretary of Defense, combatant commanders, and US military commands.

SecDef advises and assists SECSTATE and the heads of other Federal departments and agencies, as appropriate, in planning for the protection, evacuation, and repatriation of US citizens in overseas areas.

When authorized by SecDef, **Chairman of the Joint Chiefs of Staff** (CJCS) coordinates the deployment and employment of US forces in support of a NEO and monitors US force participation in the protection and evacuation of noncombatants. CJCS also recommends transportation movement priorities to SecDef and the use of United States Transportation Command (USTRANSCOM) to provide the appropriate transportation resources in support of DOS requests.

Secretary of the Army acts as the designated DOD executive agent for repatriation planning and operations, and coordinates within DOD and other USG agencies, as well as state and local agencies, as needed, in planning for the reception in the United States and onward movement of DOD dependents, nonessential DOD civilians, US nationals, and designated aliens evacuated from overseas areas.

Secretary of the Navy, in accordance with (IAW) the mission and priorities assigned by USTRANSCOM, provides military sea transportation for the evacuation of noncombatants, as required.

Secretary of the Air Force, through the Air Force Service component of USTRANSCOM, provides air transportation as well as aeromedical evacuation to support medical NEO requirements.

GCC Responsibility. IAW DOD policy, GCCs must prepare and maintain plans for the protection and evacuation of US noncombatants abroad for whom DOD is responsible.

USTRANSCOM, through its mobility components, can leverage its ability to obtain commercial lift by using existing services contracts. At a minimum, the strategic lift requirements for evacuation of noncombatants should be coordinated with USTRANSCOM.

Command and Control

Within the country, the ambassador has been designated as the responsible authority for the operation.

The US ambassador, with the approval of the Under Secretary of State for Management, can authorize the ordered or authorized departure of USG personnel and dependents other than uniformed personnel of the Armed Forces of the United States and designated emergency-essential DOD civilians who are not under the authority of the US ambassador. While the ambassador cannot order the departure of private US citizens and designated other persons, the ambassador can offer them USG evacuation assistance. Normally an evacuation starts IAW the embassy's EAP, using scheduled airlines, chartered flights, or surface transportation.

Subject to the overall authority of the ambassador, responsibility for the conduct of military operations in support of an evacuation and security of personnel, equipment, and installations within the designated operational area is vested with the JFC.

Joint task force (JTF) organization.

The supported GCC has the authority to organize forces to best accomplish the assigned mission based on the concept of operations (CONOPS). As such, the supported GCC could decide to assign the NEO mission to a Service component or establish a JTF. The JFC is responsible for all phases of the operation to include the intermediate staging base (ISB) and temporary safe haven (if located outside the United States and within the joint operations area [JOA]). An ISB or temporary safe haven outside the JTF JOA falls under the responsibility of the supported GCC. The NEO JTF is typically responsible for support and transport of the evacuees to ISBs and safe havens outside the JOA. The JFC exercises operational control over assigned and attached forces with the authority to organize forces to best accomplish the assigned tasks based on the CONOPS.

Contingency and Predeployment Planning Considerations

Emergency action plans.

US embassies and consulates are required to have EAPs for the area under their cognizance. The ambassador is responsible for the preparation and maintenance of EAPs, one section of which addresses the military evacuation of US citizens and designated foreign nationals. The GCC is responsible for reviewing and commenting on EAPs. EAPs are not tactical operation plans (OPLANs) in the sense that military planners think of, but they are the reference materials that support the formulation of an OPLAN. The GCC should review the adequacy of the EAP to support military operations. A copy of the current EAP should be on file and maintained at the appropriate GCC's headquarters (HQ).

Military planning—combatant command plans.

Predeployment planning begins when the subordinate JFC receives the warning order from the GCC and lasts until the evacuation force deploys to either an ISB or the evacuation site. Prior coordination with the staffs of the GCC and embassy can significantly improve planning for the JFC. The GCC and staff can provide the JFC with information to begin planning, such as the general OPLANs.

Notification procedures.

To develop a realistic evacuation plan, the JTF staff should know how long it will take to assemble the evacuees once the decision to evacuate has been made. Communications with potential evacuees may be via a **warden system,** which is a notification system used to communicate to the US population through wardens using telephones, faxes, e-mails, and direct personal contact. A warden coordinator prepares lists of wardens and other contacts to cover areas of assigned responsibilities. The wardens prepare, update, and maintain a list of phone numbers and addresses of US citizens residing in their assigned areas.

There are several groups of evacuees, some of whom the ambassador may direct to evacuate and some whom the ambassador cannot.

The first question most often asked by both diplomatic and military planners is, "Who are the evacuees, and how many of them will there be in a crisis?" Understanding how evacuees are organized, notified, and moved to assembly areas helps in determining the number of potential evacuees and assembly time estimates.

The report of potential evacuees, also known as the F-77 Report, identifies the numbers of potential evacuees at each embassy. Each embassy or consulate is required to submit to the DOS an annual report, on 15 December, of the estimated number of potential evacuees in its assigned area. These counts, however, are only yearly estimates. The accuracy of the estimate will vary with the speed and severity of the crisis.

Embassy security and operations.

Security outside the embassy is the responsibility of the host nation (HN), while security of the ambassador and embassy grounds is

In many cases, US embassies do not have security forces or personnel. If security is provided, the regional security officer (RSO) has DOS security personnel and a small Marine security guard (MSG) detachment to accomplish this mission. During the evacuation, the MSG detachment personnel receive their orders from the RSO, while JTF personnel receive their orders from the JFC. JTF personnel do not receive orders from the RSO. These command relationships can potentially cause problems, especially when MSG personnel and JTF personnel work together

the responsibility of the regional security officer.

during the evacuation operation. It is vital that the JTF staff work out missions and command relationships before the operation. The JFC must understand the ambassador's security plan and integrate the joint forces as smoothly as possible.

In some cases local contract guards control the perimeter of each embassy. These personnel may or may not be armed. Quality of the local guard force varies by country. Some local guards are professional and staffed with personnel who have proven their loyalty to the embassy's staff. These local guards can be very useful in assisting US forces assigned to perimeter security duty.

MSGs control access into critical facilities where classified material is processed and stored. MSGs have reaction plans to defend these facilities and destroy or evacuate sensitive material or equipment, if necessary.

Employment and Evacuation Operation Procedures

Once the Secretary of State approves an evacuation, the ambassador has the authority to implement the plan in a crisis.

DOS, acting on the advice of the ambassador, will determine when US citizens and foreign nationals are to be evacuated. When unexpected violence flares up or appears imminent and communications with DOS are cut off, the ambassador may invoke such elements of the plan and initiate such actions as the situation warrants.

Advance party.

As early as possible in the planning, the JFC forms the advance party and requests permission to send it to the site of the operation. The advance party may consist of two elements: the FCE and the evacuation site party. In a permissive or uncertain environment, the FCE should be inserted before any evacuation site parties. In a hostile environment, the ambassador's decision will probably be to insert the entire evacuation force to immediately commence the operation.

Forward command element.

The FCE coordinates with the ambassador and members of the country team for information and assistance. The FCE normally submits situation reports to the JFC. When the main body enters the country, the FCE rejoins the evacuation force and continues operations with the JTF HQ.

Evacuation site party.

The evacuation site party identifies and, where possible, establishes the assembly areas, evacuation sites, and the evacuation control center (ECC) site. When the evacuation force enters the country and the evacuation commences, the evacuation site party becomes the operations center and/or section of the ECC.

JTF main body.

A JTF "main body" will deploy to conduct the on-scene evacuation process. After insertion of the main body, each element prepares for its part in the operation. As the advance party rejoins the main body, the main body may consist of a HQ, marshalling element, security element, logistic element, and special operations forces. The size of the main body depends on the number of evacuees, evacuation sites, assembly areas, and the tactical situation.

Evacuee Processing

Evacuation control center.

The ECC supports DOS, which conducts processing, screening, and selected logistic functions associated with emergency evacuation of noncombatants. The JTF should, however, be prepared to perform functions that are DOS responsibilities, if required. Size and composition of the ECC will be determined by the number of evacuees, evacuation environment, and location of the evacuation area. Of primary importance is the nature of the emergency causing the evacuation; it may be natural, political, or military based.

Evacuee processing may take place in country at an air terminal, onboard ship, or at a temporary safe haven site. Regardless of location, a comprehensive plan for reception, accounting, and care of evacuees should be implemented. The primary duties of the commander, JTF, include maintaining order at the evacuation site and supporting the ambassador's efforts to care for noncombatant evacuees.

Guiding principles for the evacuation control center.

The three guiding principles for any ECC are accuracy—all personnel are accounted for; security—evacuees and the evacuation force are safeguarded from all threats; and speed—processing must be accomplished quickly and efficiently. As the marshalling teams bring the evacuees to the ECC, the processing center assumes control of the evacuees. The purpose is to prepare the evacuees for eventual overseas movement to a temporary safe haven or the United States. All evacuees should be screened to certify identification and to ensure that documentation is accurate and all information provided is current. The processing center performs the necessary screening, registration, medical, and transportation functions to ensure an orderly evacuation.

Intermediate Staging Base and Safe Haven Operations

An intermediate staging base is a temporary location used to stage forces prior to inserting the forces into the HN.

Use of an ISB during deployment provides the JFC many advantages over deploying directly from the home station. The ISB becomes more important as the distance from the home station increases and the likelihood of hostilities increase. The ISB may be located in another country close to where the evacuation is taking place or may be any ship under US control. Ideally, the ISB will also function as a temporary safe haven, if one is required. The ISB may also serve as an airfield for support forces, such as additional airlift for unforeseen movement requirements and/or combat forces (such as air units capable of offensive attacks and airborne infantry units) in the event that a forcible entry is required.

Temporary safe haven site.

A temporary safe haven, designated by DOS, is a location in an area or country to which evacuees may be moved quickly and easily. Ideally, the safe haven will be in the United States; however, circumstances may exist that require an intermediate or temporary safe haven. Adequate transportation may not be available to move all evacuees directly from the evacuation sites to the United States. An intermediate safe haven may be a US Navy ship; however, the evacuees should be removed from the ship to land-based safe havens (in the United States or a third country) as quickly as possible. If a temporary safe haven is required, DOS coordinates with the government in the country where it will be located. Coordination for the use of facilities, customs requirements, security, transportation, and billeting is required.

CONCLUSION

This publication provides doctrine for planning and conducting joint NEO throughout the range of military operations. Specific information on repatriation operations is also provided.

Intentionally Blank

CHAPTER I
OVERVIEW

"The people's safety is the highest law."

Legal and Political Maxim

1. Introduction

a. **Noncombatant evacuation operations (NEOs)** are conducted to assist the Department of State (DOS) in evacuating US citizens, Department of Defense (DOD) civilian personnel, and designated host nation (HN) and third country nationals (TCNs) whose lives are in danger from locations in a foreign nation to an appropriate safe haven. The United States Government (USG) will consider evacuating TCNs and host country nationals on a case-by-case, space available/reimbursable basis. Although normally considered in connection with hostile action, evacuation may also be conducted in anticipation of, or in response to, any natural or man-made disaster.

b. **US Policy**

(1) Pursuant to Executive Order 12656, *Assignment of Emergency Preparedness Responsibilities* (as amended), DOS is responsible for the protection or evacuation of US citizens and nationals abroad and for safeguarding their overseas property abroad, in consultation with the Secretaries of Defense and Health and Human Services.

(2) The US policy has resulted in a memorandum of agreement (MOA) between DOD and DOS entitled the *Memorandum of Agreement Between Departments of State and Defense on the Protection and Evacuation of US Citizens and Designated Aliens Abroad*. The MOA addresses the roles and responsibilities of each agency in implementing evacuations. DOS is responsible for the protection and evacuation of all US citizens abroad and is generally responsible for evacuating US citizens. However, under the MOA, DOS can request DOD assistance. Once the decision has been made to use military personnel and equipment to assist in the implementation of emergency evacuation plans, DOD is solely responsible for conducting the evacuation, in consultation with the principal US diplomatic or consular representative in the affected country. During an evacuation, the MOA calls for high-level coordination between DOS and DOD through a liaison group that is responsible for evacuation planning and implementation. The objectives of the MOA are summarized in Figure I-1.

c. **Characteristics.** NEOs have humanitarian, military, economic, diplomatic, and political implications. NEOs usually involve swift insertion of a force, temporary occupation of an objective, and a planned withdrawal upon completion of the mission.

OBJECTIVES CONCERNING PROTECTION AND EVACUATION OF UNITED STATES CITIZENS AND OTHER DESIGNATED PERSONNEL FROM THREATENED AREAS OVERSEAS

- Protect US citizens and nationals and designated other persons, to include, when necessary and feasible, their evacuation to and welfare in relatively safe areas.

- Reduce to a minimum the number of US citizens and nationals and designated other persons subject to the risk of death and/or seizure as hostages.

- Reduce to a minimum the number of US citizens and nationals and designated other persons in probable or actual combat areas so that combat effectiveness of US and allied forces is not impaired.

Figure I-1. Objectives Concerning Protection and Evacuation of United States Citizens and Other Designated Personnel From Threatened Areas Overseas

2. Terminology

For the purpose of simplification, the term "ambassador" is used throughout this publication. An ambassador is a diplomatic agent of the highest rank. Variations of the title ambassador or other titles referring to the senior DOS diplomatic agent or chief of mission (COM) (e.g., chargé d'affaires, consul general, or principal officer) at a particular diplomatic post could be interchanged throughout this publication and not change its relevancy.

3. Special Nature of Evacuation Operations

a. The command and control (C2) structure and the political and diplomatic factors involved in timing the execution of the military support of NEOs make them different from other military operations. During NEOs, the US ambassador, not the geographic combatant commander (GCC) or subordinate joint force commander (JFC), is the senior USG authority for the evacuation and, as such, is ultimately responsible for the successful completion of the NEO and the safety of the evacuees. The decision to evacuate a US embassy and the order to execute a NEO is political. The order to evacuate may not be given at the most opportune time, but rather may be delayed until the last possible moment to avoid actions that may be viewed as a tacit admission of political failure.

b. The GCC may decide to create a joint task force (JTF) to conduct a NEO or may task a component commander to conduct the NEO.

c. Rules of engagement (ROE) may be such that the JTF should be prepared to protect personnel (military and evacuees) from a wide variety of threats while not necessarily having the authority to preempt hostile actions by proactive military measures. The JFC influences the ROE to provide maximum flexibility to the JTF so as to not unduly restrain use of force. The JFC should be given sufficient ROE to ensure the successful accomplishment of the mission. ROE must ensure that the military commander has the authority to protect civilians while demonstrating restraint and, when appropriate, using force proportional to the threat.

See Appendix A, "Rules of Engagement and the Law of War," for additional guidance concerning ROE.

(1) Dissemination and use of clearly defined ROE are critical within all components of the JTF. Although the objectives (diplomatic and military) are not to destroy enemy forces and armed conflict should be avoided whenever possible, an appropriate and proportional use of force may become necessary. ROE must be as precise as practical; however, ROE must never deny the use of appropriate self-defense measures.

(2) The JFC shall discuss the ROE with the ambassador as early and as frequently as required. Modifications to the ROE must be made and approved by the appropriate authorities via the supported GCC.

4. Operational Environments

a. **General.** Evacuation operations are characterized by uncertainty and may be directed without warning because of sudden changes in a country's government, reoriented diplomatic or military relationships with the United States, a sudden hostile threat to US citizens from a force within or external to an HN, or a devastating natural or man-made disaster. Some key factors in noncombatant evacuation planning are situational awareness; a correct appraisal and understanding of the changing diplomatic, political, and military environment in which the evacuation force will operate; time constraints and risk; and preparation of the evacuation force for a situation that may rapidly move from permissive to uncertain or hostile. Alternative plans should be developed for permissive, uncertain, and hostile environments. Additionally, the impact of introducing US forces into an already unstable environment could be further destabilizing. As a result, a primary planning limitation may be direction from DOS to maintain a small footprint, thus limiting the level of forces or activity to the minimum required.

b. **Permissive Environment.** Under this condition, no resistance to evacuation operations is expected, and thus the operation would require little or no assembly of combat forces in country. Evacuees may or may not have been processed and assembled at designated assembly areas, evacuation points, and sites. In such an environment, a JTF can expect HN concurrence and possible support. The JTF's primary concerns may be logistic functions involving emergency medical treatment, transportation, administrative processing, and coordination with DOS and other agencies involved in the evacuation. While a minimum number of security forces may be used, prudent preparations should be in place to enable the force conducting the NEO to respond to threats as required.

c. **Uncertain Environment.** An operational environment in which host government forces, whether opposed or receptive to the NEO, do not have total effective control of the HN territory and population is an uncertain environment. Because of the uncertainty, the JFC may elect to reinforce the evacuation force with additional security units or a reaction force. Approved ROE are disseminated early to ensure that the joint force has knowledge of and is sufficiently trained and proficient in application of the ROE. Planning for NEOs conducted in an uncertain environment must always include the possibility for escalation to a hostile environment. The primary concerns associated with a permissive environment remain unchanged.

d. **Hostile Environment.** Noncombatants may be evacuated under conditions ranging from civil disorder, to terrorist action, to full-scale combat. Under such conditions, the JTF must be prepared for a wide range of contingencies. The JFC may elect to deploy a sizable security element with the evacuation force or position a large reaction force, either with the evacuation force or at an intermediate staging base (ISB). In addition to normal functions associated with noncombatant evacuations (embarkation, transportation, medical, and services), the JTF may be required to conduct a forcible entry operation, establish defensive perimeters, escort convoys, participate in personnel recovery (PR) operations, and perform the screening of evacuees normally accomplished by DOS officials.

5. Military Planning and Forces

a. Department of Defense Directive (DODD) 3025.14, *Protection and Evacuation of US Citizens and Designated Aliens in Danger Areas Abroad*, assigns the responsibility to plan and conduct NEOs in support of DOS to the GCCs. Actual evacuation assistance can be provided only upon the request of the Secretary of State (SECSTATE) to either the Secretary of Defense (SecDef) or the President. Once requested, approved, and directed, the combatant commander (CCDR) will order assigned and/or attached forces to conduct evacuation operations in support of DOS and the US ambassador. The ambassador is not in the military chain of command, but as the senior US official on scene is responsible for the NEO and protection of US citizens, citizens of the HN, or TCNs who have been designated for evacuation. It is imperative that the ambassador's evacuation plan and the JFC's plan for the NEO be supportive, coordinated, and fully integrated.

b. **Military Response.** Normally, the JFC or a Service component commander will receive authorization from the supported GCC before using any forces and facilities in a foreign country for protection and evacuation. However, if a JFC or Service component commander receives a request from the ambassador or responsible US diplomatic representative to provide assistance and the delay in obtaining authorization would jeopardize the safety of US citizens, the JFC or Service component commander should respond to the extent deemed necessary and militarily feasible and notify the supported and supporting CCDRs of contemplated actions.

c. **Force Options and Considerations**

(1) **Force options** to conduct a NEO may, first and foremost, **depend on the operational environment** in which the NEO will be conducted. Many of the GCC's

THIRD COUNTRY NATIONALS

Current policy on third country nationals is outlined in the Department of State's (DOS's) 12 Foreign Affairs Handbook-1, *Emergency Planning Handbook*. Essentially this provision states that in the event of a noncombatant evacuation operation (NEO), the United States Government (USG) will consider extending—on a humanitarian, space available but reimbursable basis—evacuation assistance to foreign nationals.

In practice, we have repeatedly assisted virtually all governments requesting assistance in evacuating their nationals from countries in which a NEO has become necessary.

DOS refrains from entering into formal agreements with other governments on the evacuation of their nationals. We have two long-standing agreements with the Canadians and British to consult with each other with respect to evacuation planning. All foreign governments (including Canadian and British) are urged to plan for their own nationals' evacuation and not to depend on USG resources.

Memorandum of Agreement Between Departments of State and Defense on the Protection and Evacuation of US Citizens and Designated Aliens Abroad

components are capable of conducting a NEO in a permissive environment. However, a NEO in an uncertain or hostile environment may require formation and deployment of a JTF. An exception to this is the forward-deployed amphibious ready group (ARG)/Marine expeditionary unit (MEU), which is trained and certified to conduct NEOs. A sea base may also be established to support a NEO. The sea base can include the ARG/MEU, or consist of other forces, both US and multinational, as needed to accomplish the mission. For a large-scale NEO, forces from other components and supporting CCDRs will normally be required.

(2) **The HN's support capabilities may play a major role** in determining courses of action (COAs) for the conduct of NEOs. The supported GCC should consider a flexible force option that provides both early response to a developing situation and a capability to quickly expand should the operational environment become hostile. To provide the smallest opportunity to a potential adversary, **evacuation forces entering foreign territory should be kept to the minimum number required** for self-defense and for extraction and protection of evacuees, and for accomplishing the normal functions associated with noncombatant evacuations. The GCC may initiate a joint sea base to provide the required NEO capability from international waters, while minimizing the footprint ashore.

(3) **Command of the Joint Task Force.** Military forces employed in a NEO may be composed of units from more than one Service. Once ordered to support a NEO and following the supported GCC's decision to employ a JTF, **a JFC will be designated to exercise overall control of operations.**

For additional guidance on JTF headquarters (HQ) functions, refer to Joint Publication (JP) 3-33, Joint Task Force Headquarters.

      (4) **Force Sequencing.** Force sequencing is the phased introduction of forces into and out of the operational area. **Force sequencing provides the JFC with the option to provide a flexible and rapid response to a NEO** through employment of forward-deployed forces, which may form the nucleus for a larger tailored force to be deployed from an ISB. Effective force sequencing requires detailed knowledge of available Service, joint, and multinational military capabilities. Force sequencing is frequently discussed in terms of the time-phased force and deployment data (TPFDD). The TPFDD contains time-phased force data, movement data, and non-unit related cargo and personnel data for the operation plan (OPLAN).

      d. **Multinational Forces (MNFs).** In planning for a NEO, the ambassador, GCC, and JFC may consider the possibility of operating with MNFs. However, the approval for US participation in a multinational NEO will come only from the President of the United States. When the NEO is to evacuate US citizens and nationals and designated other persons abroad using an MNF, SECSTATE may approve the use of an MNF. Under an emergency situation involving the safety of human life or the protection of property, offers of voluntary service from other countries may be accepted prior to approval.

      (1) Many situations that would cause the United States to initiate a NEO would likely cause other countries to react similarly. **It may be politically or militarily expedient to employ an MNF in conducting the operation.** These may be either HN forces cooperating in the evacuation or third nation forces whose citizens are also threatened.

      (2) The use of an MNF in a potential NEO should be a planning consideration. If seriously contemplated, detailed multinational planning and rehearsal are important factors in ensuring a successful operation. **The difficulties of obtaining unity of effort within an MNF may cause serious difficulties in a time-sensitive NEO.**

      (3) Other nations' forces need not be integrated with US forces unless diplomatic considerations recommend such action or in the event that the other nations' forces have trained and operated with US forces. Although the United States may elect not to operate with MNFs directly, coordination and deconfliction with other countries involved in NEOs is essential. The JFC should consider an exchange of liaison officers (LNOs) with all other countries involved in their own NEO to facilitate coordination and deconfliction of effort. Consequently, GCCs should consider pre-NEO coordination with partner nations to facilitate such coordination and deconfliction.

CHAPTER II
ROLES, COORDINATION, AND INTERACTION

> *"As specified in EO [Executive Order] 12656, the Secretary of Defense shall advise and assist the Secretary of State and the heads of other federal departments and agencies, as appropriate, in planning for the protection, evacuation, and repatriation of US citizens in overseas areas."*
>
> **Department of Defense Directive 3025.14, *Protection and Evacuation of US Citizens and Designated Aliens in Danger Areas Abroad (Short Title: Noncombatant Evacuation Operations)***

1. Introduction

This chapter discusses the roles and responsibilities of principal persons and organizations, whether governmental, civil, intergovernmental, or military, with whom the JFC may interact while planning or executing a NEO. Additionally, specific roles and responsibilities that these organizations may have for repatriation operations are found later in this chapter and Chapter III, "Command and Control."

For further information on other USG, nongovernmental organizations' (NGOs'), and intergovernmental organizations' (IGOs') roles and responsibilities, refer to JP 3-08, Interorganizational Coordination During Joint Operations.

2. Department of State

a. At all levels, DOD and DOS personnel need to cooperate to successfully execute the NEO. This is most important at the ambassador and JFC level and includes their staffs and all other personnel. While the protection of US citizens being evacuated remains paramount, NEOs will probably be conducted in an environment where political concerns and constraints are key considerations. In most cases, the United States may not be actively engaged militarily against the forces posing a threat to the noncombatants. Military action may therefore be limited by the situation. Political and diplomatic constraints may also be imposed on the introduction of military personnel into a country prior to an evacuation operation, thus hampering planning and preparation. The JFC will fully support the ambassador's plans and cooperate with DOS and embassy personnel without compromising mission requirements. DOS and embassy personnel will keep the JFC fully apprised of the on-scene conditions and are influential for coordinating actions that greatly affect the NEO. These actions include political and diplomatic influences on the JFC's legal issues, agreements, rights, privileges, and immunities (if any) within the HN, the ISB, and the safe haven.

b. **Washington Liaison Group (WLG).** SECSTATE and SecDef established the WLG to ensure coordination of the work of their departments in fulfilling their responsibilities for protection and evacuation of US citizens abroad. **The WLG is responsible for coordination and implementation at the national level of all emergency and evacuation**

plans by DOS and DOD and by other USG agencies as appropriate. The WLG is chaired by a DOS representative. The WLG may invite representatives of other USG departments and agencies (e.g., Department of Health and Human Services [DHHS], Department of Homeland Security [DHS] [US Coast Guard], Federal Bureau of Investigation, Central Intelligence Agency, United States Agency for International Development [USAID]) to participate in its meetings or attend as observers. The representatives on the WLG are the points of contact for their department or agency on all matters pertaining to emergency evacuation planning, implementation of plans, and coordination of repatriation activities. To fulfill its responsibilities, the WLG:

(1) Recommends the establishment of such regional liaison groups (RLGs) as are advisable, along with their terms of reference, to SECSTATE.

(2) Provides advice on evacuation planning and protection of US citizens and TCNs and designated other persons to RLGs, US diplomatic and consular posts, and military commands in country.

(3) Monitors the activities of the RLGs and provides direction as required through appropriate channels.

(4) Periodically reviews protection and evacuation capabilities relative to the number of US citizens and TCNs and designated other persons throughout the world.

(5) Coordinates operations of DOD and DOS incident to the evacuation and/or in-place protection of US citizens and nationals and designated other persons abroad and the use of the DOD noncombatant evacuee accountability system. Upon activation of the SecDef Crisis Coordination Center and/or the Joint Chiefs of Staff crisis response elements within the National Military Command Center during an emergency or actual evacuation, the WLG's responsibilities for coordination of the operations of DOD and DOS during the crisis may be discharged through these elements together with the respective task force or working group within the DOS Operations Center.

c. **Regional Liaison Groups.** SECSTATE and SecDef have established RLGs colocated with combatant commands as necessary to ensure coordination of emergency and evacuation planning by their departments in the field. Each RLG is chaired by a DOS representative. Membership includes representatives of the appropriate CCDR and any subordinate component commands as desired. The RLG may invite representatives of other USG departments and agencies to participate in its meetings when appropriate and useful. The chairperson of each RLG receives instructions from SECSTATE. Each RLG performs the following functions.

(1) Provides support to officials at diplomatic and consular posts and military commands within its region by:

(a) Providing liaison between the WLG and the posts.

(b) Ensuring coordination exists between the various posts, and between the posts and appropriate military commands.

(c) Assisting posts and appropriate military commands in planning for the evacuation and/or in-place protection of US citizens, HN nationals or TCNs, and designated other persons in an emergency.

(d) Reviewing the emergency action plans (EAPs) created on the Crisis and Emergency Planning Application that are prepared by posts. Forward them to DOS for approval and distribution to ensure the information contained therein is adequate to meet the requirements of DOS and DOD, review post plans and US and allied military OPLANs to determine if they conflict, and ensure plans of all posts in the area are coordinated when necessary.

(2) Refers to the WLG relevant issues that cannot be resolved.

(3) The military members of each regional group shall receive their instructions from SecDef through the appropriate GCC.

d. **Emergency Action Committee (EAC).** This organization is established at a foreign service post by the ambassador for the purpose of directing and coordinating the post's response to contingencies as well as drafting the post's EAP. The EAC is the focal point for DOS and DOD evacuation site interface. Another important aspect of the EAC mission is to brief, coordinate, and plan for the evacuation or protection of US noncombatants and certain TCNs or HN nationals in a crisis, whether by regular commercial, chartered, or US military transportation. The EAC normally is composed of representatives of each USG and foreign affairs agency present at the post or under the authority of the ambassador, and would most likely include the senior defense official/defense attaché (SDO/DATT) and/or the chief of the military mission.

3. United States Embassy Representatives

a. Joint forces involved in NEOs should familiarize themselves with the duties of the following positions normally found at US embassies and/or missions.

b. **Ambassador.** The ambassador is the personal representative of the President to the government of the foreign country or to the IGO to which he or she is accredited and, as such, is the COM, responsible for recommending and implementing national policy regarding the foreign country or IGO and for overseeing the activities of USG employees in the mission. The President with the advice and consent of the Senate appoints the ambassador. The ambassador has extraordinary decision-making authority as the senior USG official on the ground during crises.

c. **Deputy Chief of Mission (DCM).** The DCM is chosen from the ranks of career foreign service officers through a rigorous selection process to be the principal deputy to the ambassador. Although not appointed by the President with the advice and consent of the

Senate, the DCM wields considerable power, especially when acting as the COM while in chargé status.

d. **United States Defense Attaché Office (USDAO).** The USDAO is an office of Service attachés managed by the Defense Intelligence Agency. A US SDO/DATT heads the defense attaché office (DAO) in country and is a member of the country team. The SDO/DATT is the COM's principal military advisor on defense and national security issues, the senior diplomatically accredited DOD military officer assigned to a US diplomatic mission, and the single point of contact (POC) for all DOD matters involving the embassy or DOD elements assigned to or working from the embassy. The DATT is normally the senior Service attaché assigned to the mission. The SDO/DATT is the in-country focal point for planning, coordinating, and executing support to USG officials for in-country US defense issues and activities that are not under the purview of the parent DOD components. The attachés serve as liaisons with their HN counterparts and are valuable sources of information for the COM and GCC on the military affairs of the HN. The DATT may be accredited to more than one country. The SDO/DATT is also the in-country representative of SecDef, the Chairman of the Joint Chiefs of Staff (CJCS), and the GCC and is responsible (under the direction of the COM) for coordinating administrative and security matters for all DOD elements assigned to the country, except those under the control of a GCC. The attachés assist in the foreign internal defense program by exchanging information with the GCC's staff on HN military, political, humanitarian, religious, social, and economic conditions and interagency coordination.

e. **Security Assistance Officer (SAO).** The SAO maintains liaison with the HN military forces and is authorized by law to perform certain military functions with the HN military. The advance party forward command element (FCE) should coordinate with the SAO. JFCs should be cognizant that not all embassies have an SAO; rather, some may have a DAO or no military personnel at all. In many countries, security assistance functions are performed within the DAO. The SAO—which may comprise a military assistance advisory group, another military activity, or a SAO—operates under the direction of the COM but reports administratively to the GCC and is funded by the Defense Security Cooperation Agency. The SAO assists HN security forces by planning and administering military aspects of the security assistance program. The SAO also helps the country team communicate HN assistance needs to policy and budget officials within the USG. In addition, the SAO provides oversight of training and assistance teams temporarily assigned to the HN.

f. **Chief of Station (COS).** As the senior intelligence advisor to the ambassador, the COS is an excellent source of information on the country and the current situation. As senior intelligence advisor, the COS should provide an updated threat description for the proposed NEO.

g. **Administration Officer.** The administration officer is responsible for various activities at the embassy compound(s), which may include security at small posts; running the commissary, motor pool, and maintenance activities; and handling monetary aspects of embassy business, including foreign service national payroll, cash collection, and the budget. At a small post with no security officer assigned, the administration officer assumes the functions of the post security officer (PSO) and has operational control (OPCON) of the Marine security guard (MSG) detachment. Because of his frequent dealings with HN businesspeople, the administration officer is an excellent source of information on local indigenous personnel.

(1) **General Services Officer (GSO).** The GSO works for the administration officer and is responsible for buildings, grounds, construction, vehicles, and maintenance.

(2) **Information Management Officer (IMO).** Formerly called the communications project officer, the IMO runs the post communications center, processes and tracks all classified pouch material, and oversees the computer system at the embassy. The IMO is the POC concerning the communication capabilities available at the post.

h. **Political Officer.** The political officer reports on political developments, negotiates with the host government, and represents views and policies of the USG. The political officer maintains regular contact with host government officials, political and labor leaders, and other influential citizens of the HN, as well as other countries' diplomats. The political officer is a major contributor to the overall intelligence picture.

i. **Commercial and/or Economic Officer.** The commercial and/or economic officer analyzes, reports on, and advises superiors, DOS, and DOD personnel on economic matters in the HN. Economic officers also negotiate with the host government on trade and financial issues.

j. **Consular Officer.** The consular officer's major role is to screen, process, and grant US passports and visas. Other responsibilities the consular officer may be assigned include attending to the welfare of US citizens and administrative tasks such as maintaining a census of US nationals within the HN. The consular officer provides the requisite number of personnel needed to screen documents of all potential evacuees during a NEO and provides instructions to any evacuation control center (ECC) personnel needed to staff processing stations. In countries where thousands or tens of thousands have to be evacuated in a short period due to high risk, the US embassy will not have adequate in-house consular capabilities. The US embassy may have to request support from DOS to obtain additional consular personnel to assist in processing. This is in addition to task organizing embassy personnel to fulfill requirements.

k. **Regional Medical Officer.** The regional medical officer is qualified for general practice and is trained to set up triage, trauma, and mass casualty operations. The regional medical officer may also advise the JFC on indigenous diseases and proper preventative procedures for forces executing the NEO.

l. **Regional Security Officer (RSO).** The RSO is a DOS security officer responsible for the security functions of all US embassies and consulates in a given country or group of adjacent countries. The RSO provides direction to the MSG detachment via the detachment commander. The RSO oversees the following personnel:

(1) **Post Security Officer.** Posts with no RSO have a PSO. The PSO has general security duties at a specific embassy (or consulate) and is usually the administration officer.

(2) **Mobile Security Division (MSD).** The MSD consists of DOS employees of the Diplomatic Security Service who respond to crises in foreign countries. The MSD is trained to respond to increased threats or critical security needs at an embassy, provide additional security, and provide immediate response to a security-related incident.

m. **Public Affairs Officer (PAO).** The PAO is the ambassador's advisor concerning public affairs (PA) and overseer of US cultural center operations. The PAO will be responsible for all press releases and press inquiries for information directed to the embassy. The PAO usually speaks at press conferences when the ambassador is unable to attend.

n. **United States Marine Corps Security Guard Detachment.** A MSG detachment will have a minimum of six Marines, with the maximum number assigned dictated by need. The Marine detachment commander is normally a member of the EAC and is responsible to the RSO or PSO for internal security and protection of classified material and US personnel assigned to the embassy. Administrative control of detachment Marines is through the regional Marine officer (RMO). This detachment remains part of the embassy security force and normally will not be subsumed under JFC control.

o. **Country Team.** The interdepartmental country team consists of key members of the US diplomatic mission or embassy that work directly with the HN government. Its purpose is to unify the coordination and implementation of US national policy within each foreign country under direction of the ambassador. The country team meets regularly to advise the ambassador on matters of interest to the United States and reviews current developments in the country.

(1) The country team members usually include those shown in Figure II-1.

(2) One aim of the country team focus is to direct attention toward identification of potential sources of conflict and threats to US interests in a country and to minimize problems by introducing programs designed to assist the economy, enhance medical care, and improve the infrastructure of the country.

p. **DOD Force Protection Detachments (FPDs).** The primary mission of DOD FPDs is to detect and warn of threats to DOD personnel (military, civilian, and dependents) and resources in-transit at overseas locations without a permanent DOD counterintelligence (CI) presence. FPDs serve as force protection multipliers for the US embassy country team in support of the DOD presence in those overseas locations.

4. Other Agencies

During NEOs, the JFC will probably be required to coordinate with agencies outside DOS. Other agencies that may have important responsibilities during NEOs include the following:

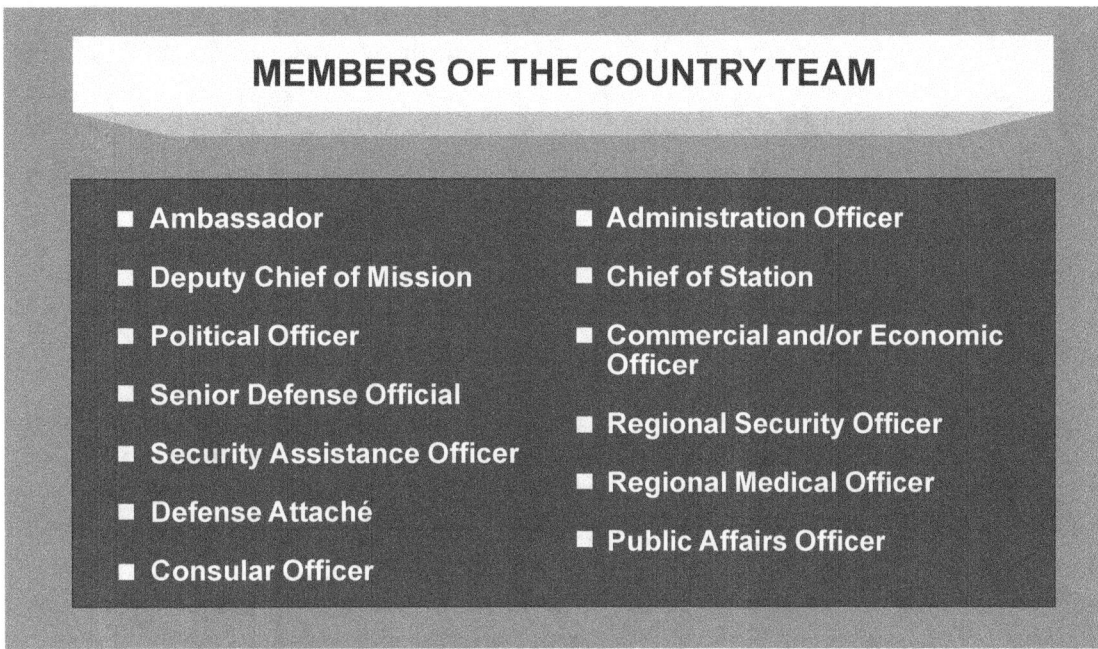

Figure II-1. Members of the Country Team

a. **US Agency for International Development.** USAID is an autonomous agency under the policy direction of SECSTATE. It plays a vital role in promoting US national security and foreign policy. USAID promotes peace and stability by fostering economic growth, protecting human health, providing emergency humanitarian assistance, and enhancing democracy in developing countries. Administratively, it functions within DOS and operates under an administrator who also serves as the special coordinator for international disaster assistance. USAID administers and directs the US foreign economic assistance program and acts as the lead federal agency (LFA) for US foreign disaster assistance. USAID works largely in support of DOS and manages a worldwide network of country programs for economic and policy reforms that generates sound economic growth, encourages political freedom and good governance, and invests in human resource development. Responding to natural and man-made disasters is one of USAID's primary missions.

b. **Department of Health and Human Services.** By law (Title 42 US Code, Section 1313) and Executive Order 12656, *Assignment of Emergency Preparedness Responsibilities*, the DHHS is the LFA for the reception of all evacuees in the United States. DHHS personnel meet and assist evacuees at the US port of entry. Their plans rely on state and local governments to carry out the operational responsibilities of repatriation. In wartime, the *DHHS Repatriation Plan* as governed by Executive Order 12656 will be implemented. In nonemergency conditions, the embassy and DOS will coordinate DHHS assistance rendered to evacuees.

c. **United States Citizenship and Immigration Services (USCIS).** The USCIS is part of the DHS. If the United States is designated as the safe haven, the USCIS may meet evacuees at the port of entry. USCIS representatives in country can assist in identifying the foreign nationals to be evacuated. Responsibilities of the USCIS include the following:

(1) Facilitate the entry of legally admissible persons as visitors or as immigrants to the United States.

(2) Adjudication of immigrant visa petitions.

(3) Adjudication of naturalization petitions.

(4) Adjudication of asylum and refugee applications.

d. **National Geospatial-Intelligence Agency (NGA).** NGA support teams (NSTs) provide a strong forward presence and have been very successful in supporting geospatial intelligence (GEOINT) operations at National System for Geospatial Intelligence (NSG) partner sites. They can provide timely, relevant, and accurate GEOINT in direct support of NEOs. NGA provides on-site GEOINT products, services, and direct representational authority, in cooperation with NSG mission partners, to the mission partner along a continuum of support, the basis of which is the cross-functional NST, composed of analysts, technicians, staff officers, and managers. The NST chief or senior NGA representative is designated by the Director, NGA, as the senior representative to the mission partner's commander or director and is the primary POC for all GEOINT support provided by NGA at the site.

For information on NGA capabilities and NSTs, see JP 2-03, Geospatial Intelligence Support to Joint Operations.

5. Secretary of Defense, Combatant Commanders, and United States Military Commands

a. **Secretary of Defense.** SecDef advises and assists SECSTATE and the heads of other Federal departments and agencies, as appropriate, in planning for the protection, evacuation, and repatriation of US citizens in overseas areas. SecDef has primary responsibility for the protection and evacuation of US noncombatants at the US Naval Base, Guantanamo Bay, Cuba.

b. **Chairman of the Joint Chiefs of Staff.** When authorized by SecDef, CJCS coordinates the deployment and employment of US forces in support of a NEO and monitors US force participation in the protection and evacuation of noncombatants. CJCS also recommends transportation movement priorities to SecDef and the use of United States Transportation Command (USTRANSCOM) to provide the appropriate transportation resources in support of DOS requests. In addition, the CJCS coordinates with the Secretaries of the Military Departments and CCDRs on evacuee personnel accounting actions.

c. **Secretary of the Army (SECARMY).** SECARMY acts as the designated DOD executive agent for repatriation planning and operations, and coordinates within DOD and other USG agencies, as well as state and local agencies, as needed, in planning for the reception in the United States and onward movement of DOD dependents, nonessential DOD civilians, US nationals, and designated aliens evacuated from overseas areas. Also, SECARMY is responsible for establishing and operating a joint reception coordination center (JRCC) and managing all of the DOD noncombatants' needs as specified in the *Joint Plan for DOD Noncombatant Repatriation (Non-Emergency)*.

d. **Secretary of the Navy (SECNAV).** SECNAV, in accordance with (IAW) the mission and priorities assigned by USTRANSCOM, provides military sea transportation for the evacuation of noncombatants, as required. Also, SECNAV provides augmentation support to the JRCC, when requested, including appropriate Marine Corps and, if transferred to Navy operational control, Coast Guard resources. Further, SECNAV monitors all Department of the Navy noncombatants when evacuated to a safe haven.

e. **Secretary of the Air Force (SECAF).** SECAF, through the Air Force Service component of USTRANSCOM, provides air transportation as well as aeromedical evacuation (AE) to support medical NEO requirements. Also, SECAF provides augmentation support to the JRCC, when requested, and monitors all Department of the Air Force noncombatants when evacuated to a safe haven.

f. **Geographic Combatant Commander Responsibility.** IAW DOD policy, GCCs must prepare and maintain plans for the protection and evacuation of US noncombatants abroad for whom DOD is responsible. Plans will include the evacuation of military personnel not included in consular and/or embassy plans. Plans will also include identification of emergency-essential civilians operating in support of combat units who will not be evacuated. When conditions of potential hazard warrant, the GCC will recommend evacuation of DOD noncombatants to the CJCS, and the GCC may direct that DOD personnel under his control be evacuated from a foreign nation to an appropriate safe haven when authorized by SecDef in coordination with SECSTATE.

g. **Special Responsibilities of the Commander, US Northern Command (CDRUSNORTHCOM), Commander, US Pacific Command (CDRUSPACOM), and Commander, US Southern Command (CDRUSSOUTHCOM).** Under conditions of a nonemergency evacuation, CDRUSNORTHCOM, CDRUSPACOM, and CDRUSSOUTHCOM are the safe haven commanders for DOD repatriation in their respective areas of responsibility (AORs). Additionally, CDRUSPACOM is responsible for repatriation operations in Hawaii and US territories in the Pacific. While the Department of Army is the DOD executive agent for repatriation of DOD noncombatant evacuees, CDRUSNORTHCOM may provide repatriation services to non-DOD personnel for the continental United States (CONUS), Alaska, Canada, Puerto Rico, US Virgin Islands, Mexico, Bahamas, British Virgin Islands, and Turks and Caicos Islands. CDRUSSOUTHCOM is responsible for repatriation operations within the designated AOR.

h. **Commander, US Coast Guard Atlantic Area, and Commander, US Coast Guard Pacific Area.** Due to its reputation as a humanitarian Service, the Coast Guard may be called upon to play a vital role in certain emergency evacuation situations. The relatively nonbelligerent nature of Coast Guard cutters and aircraft make them an option in cases where a DOD presence may exacerbate a potentially hostile situation.

i. **Special Responsibilities of the Commander, United States Special Operations Command (CDRUSSOCOM).** As a member of the WLG, the special operations forces (SOF) representative coordinates with DOS, the GCCs, and the Services to ensure the adequacy and timeliness of special operations planning and coordination in support of NEOs.

j. **Commander, US Transportation Command.** USTRANSCOM, through its mobility components, can leverage its ability to obtain commercial lift by using existing services contracts. Additionally, USTRANSCOM will have visibility over unused legs of contracted missions which can be obtained quickly and converted to round trip at minimal cost, thereby flowing evacuation missions with other scheduled commercial missions. At a minimum, the strategic lift requirements for evacuation of noncombatants should be coordinated with USTRANSCOM.

k. **Marine Corps Security Force Regiment (MCSFR).** The MCSFR has three fleet antiterrorism security team (FAST) companies totaling 18 platoons of one officer and 45 enlisted Marines and one Navy corpsman each. These FAST platoons can provide a rapidly deployable augmentation of the MSG, providing the CCDR and ambassador with a low-visibility reinforcement capability. MCSFR and its assets are OPCON to respective fleet commanders if currently deployed. If not deployed, all MCSFR assets fall under Marine Forces Command.

l. **Regional Marine Officer.** The RMO is the company commander of the MSGs within a specific geographic region.

m. **Defense Manpower Data Center (DMDC).** The DMDC is a component of the DOD field activity, Department of Defense Human Resources Activity. DMDC has two responsibilities associated with a NEO conducted by DOD: the centralized procurement and distribution of NEO tracking system (NTS) to a geographic combatant command and the maintenance of the DMDC NTS Web site at https://www.dmdc.osd.mil/nts during the conduct of a NEO.

n. **Comptroller of the Department of Defense.** The DOD Comptroller establishes financial arrangements with DOS and issues instructions to the DOD components for obtaining reimbursement for the costs of protecting and evacuating personnel for whom DOD is not responsible. When DOS incurs expenses for personnel for whom DOD is responsible, the DOD Comptroller completes arrangements for the reimbursement of costs.

6. **Host Nation**

a. **Political and Legal Considerations.** Coordination and interaction with the HN and en route HN governments will be required to determine, among other things, legal authority to conduct a NEO, overflight rights, ROE constraints due to HN laws, status of international agreements (e.g., status-of-forces agreement [SOFA], memorandums of understanding [MOUs]), request and/or approval for and NEO-related intelligence collection activities, and the legal status of evacuation force personnel. The outcome of this effort will influence the level of freedom and ease with which the evacuation force may execute its mission.

See Appendix B, "Legal Considerations," for further guidance.

b. **Actions.** The response and activities of the HN during a NEO likely will be determined by the existing operational environment—permissive, uncertain, or hostile. The HN may assist the NEO by providing security outside the embassy property, around evacuation sites, and along evacuation routes. Continuous liaison and coordination between the embassy RSO and local police/military force commanders likely will be required to ensure this support is established and maintained. The HN also may be capable and willing to provide interpreters and intelligence, logistic, and communications support to the embassy staff and evacuation force. Other host-nation support (HNS) such as traffic control, airspace control, and port operations likely will be vital to NEO execution relieving the burden on the evacuation force.

7. Nongovernmental and Intergovernmental Organizations

a. NGOs are organizations that may be in a country providing humanitarian assistance or relief when an evacuation takes place. They also may voluntarily assist dislocated civilians during all or selected stages of NEO. Approximately 350 agencies capable of conducting some form of humanitarian relief operation are registered with USAID. USAID publishes a yearly report, titled *Voluntary Foreign Aid Programs,* that describes the aims and objectives of the registered organizations. The JTF should be cautioned that personnel working for these organizations cannot be ordered to leave a country. However, they may be able to provide valuable up-to-date information as to the location of US citizens. Some of these agencies or organizations may not support US goals. An early determination of their position in relation to US policy is essential.

b. **Regional and Intergovernmental Organizations.** Regional organizations or IGOs may provide assistance to refugees during a US evacuation from a foreign country.

See JP 3-08, Interorganizational Coordination During Joint Operations, *for more information on coordination with NGOs and IGOs. JP 3-08 also provides a discussion on relationships between the Armed Forces of the US and NGOs and IGOs.*

8. Multinational Noncombatant Evacuation Operation

a. **Initiation.** Multinational evacuations involve multiple nation diplomatic initiatives—with coalition/combined forces conducting a NEO in a supporting role. A political decision from each of the participating nations is required to conduct a NEO with an MNF. However, military-to-military engagement can be conducted to facilitate unilateral national NEOs, so long as no formal agreements are initiated—because binding agreements fall under the auspices of DOS. Should the political powers decide on a requirement for a multinational NEO, an initiating directive (ID) should be issued to enable detailed operational planning to commence. The ID establishes the authority and parameters for the NEO. An ID normally includes guidance regarding the situation, political objectives, mission, participating nations, and timing. Specific guidance on conducting NEOs within the North Atlantic Treaty Organization (NATO) is provided in Allied Joint Publication (AJP)-3.4.2, *Allied Joint Doctrine for Noncombatant Evacuation Operations.*

b. **Command and Control**

(1) Subject to the overall authority of the ambassador(s), the multinational force commander (MNFC) is responsible for the conduct of military operations in support of an evacuation, and for the security of personnel, equipment, and installations within the assigned operational area. Although the ambassador(s) is the responsible national authority for a NEO, during a multinational NEO the MNF conducts operations in response to ID guidance—the ambassador(s) does not exercise military command over the MNF. In cases when significant differences between the MNFC and an ambassador become an obstacle to success of the operation, they will seek resolution from their respective superiors.

(2) The primary goal of the MNFC is to support the ambassadors' plans and cooperate with the diplomatic missions without compromising military mission requirements. The diplomatic missions can keep the MNF apprised of the on-scene conditions and can be influential for coordinating actions that may affect the NEO. These actions may include political or diplomatic constraints on the joint force, legal issues, agreements, rights, privileges, and immunities (if any) within the HN, an ISB, and a temporary safe haven, if established.

(3) Depending on the magnitude and anticipated duration of a NEO, the MNFC may request designation of a **coordinated lead diplomatic mission** within the HN. Such a request would need to be discussed and agreed upon within the national foreign ministries. A designated coordinated lead diplomatic mission should have sufficient personnel and C2 assets to serve as a focal point for coordinating NEO efforts among the alliance/coalition and other diplomatic missions included for evacuation. The intent of creating a coordinated lead diplomatic mission is to foster a degree of unity of effort and lessen the liaison burden on the MNF.

c. **Liaison.** An MNF LNO and reconnaissance team (i.e., FCE) should be deployed to act as a link between the MNFC and the ambassador and gather information. In addition to information gathering, the early deployment of LNOs to the HN should be considered to:

(1) Brief the ambassador(s) on NEO procedures, the likely forces involved, and other military considerations.

(2) Coordinate with the military attachés and staffs, the diplomatic mission staffs, HN military, and the military personnel or forces of other nations deployed in the operational area.

(3) Review the evacuation plans and coordinate with military plans.

(4) Commence NEO planning to include initiating the commander's estimate and OPLAN on behalf of the MNFC and the tactical planning for the MNF components.

(5) Compile local information not otherwise available.

(6) Test or provide a communications system at the diplomatic mission.

d. **Organization**

(1) **General Composition.** The MNF will be a task-organized tailored force whose composition will be determined mostly by the needs of the entry/withdrawal and supporting operations within the overall NEO. Typically, the MNF will consist of an MNF HQ and functional components.

(2) **Operational Elements.** The MNF likely will task-organize to form an **advance HQ, main body, and evacuation force.** The advance HQ coordinates with the ambassador(s) and diplomatic mission staff(s) for information and assistance. The advance HQ reports to the MNFC. The MNF "main body" HQ joins the advance HQ as operations continue, and it coordinates and directs the MNF components during the NEO. The LNOs continue to coordinate directly with the diplomatic missions and other agencies as required. **In most instances, the evacuation force is established from a designated MNF component, with other MNF components in a supporting role.** For instance, if the NEO is permissive or uncertain with noncombatants departing primarily by air, the joint force air component commander may be designated the evacuation force commander.

(3) **Noncombatant Evacuation Operation Coordination Center (NEOCC).** Depending on the magnitude and duration of the multinational NEO, the MNFC might consider establishing a NEOCC within the MNF HQ. The purpose of the NEOCC would be to create a centralized focal point providing a conduit for information exchanges between the various diplomatic missions and the MNF.

e. **Planning**

(1) Review all available evacuation contingency plans, to include the mission's EAP.

(2) Perform a commander's estimate. Note: A sample NEO estimate is contained in Annex B, Sample Noncombatant Evacuation Operations Estimate Format, of AJP-3.4.2, *Allied Joint Doctrine for Noncombatant Evacuation Operations.*

(3) Obtain through direct liaison(s) the unique constraints and restraints (e.g., regarding the use of force), security plans, procedures for "walk-ins," and plans for the protection/evacuation/destruction of classified material from the ambassador(s) relevant to the MNF's assistance.

(4) Develop/modify an OPLAN through the appropriate alliance/coalition process.

f. **Execution.** A multinational NEO may be conducted in four phases—**preparatory operations, preliminary operations, evacuation operations, and withdrawal and redeployment.** These phases are usually sequential, but may have significant overlap.

(1) **Preparatory Operations.** Activities during this phase include gathering intelligence, generating the MNF, training and rehearsals, logistic buildup, and other administrative preparations.

(2) **Preliminary Operations.** During this phase the MNF will likely deploy to a secure ISB(s), identify evacuation points, and assist in the establishment of the ECC as required. If the NEO is conducted in a hostile environment this phase may include forcible entry operations or operations to shape the operational environment.

(3) **Evacuation Operations.** The main effort during this phase is the safe and swift evacuation of evacuees enabled by a rapid insertion of the MNF. The MNF should secure vital areas; support reception centers, ECCs, and embarkation points; evacuate the noncombatants; and provide force protection.

(4) **Withdrawal and Redeployment.** The military end state for a NEO is the safe evacuation of all noncombatants to designated safe havens and the withdrawal of the MNF. Thereafter, redeployment to home station or to other tasks will normally occur.

g. **Logistics**

(1) **Support.** NEOs, by their very nature, normally occur in nations where there seldom is a logistic support structure established by one or any of the allies or coalition partners. Therefore, **the only guarantee of sufficient logistic support is if the MNF provides its own or makes solid short-notice, in-country support arrangements.** A logistic estimate must be conducted to ascertain requirements. Although not an exhaustive list, some of the support arrangements that could be established are as follows:

(a) If a legitimate government exists, and there is sufficient time to negotiate an agreement, the implementation of HNS under an umbrella MOU can be arranged.

(b) In cases where an HNS agreement is not practical, resources may still be obtained locally. In-country resources, in the form of local contracts, can be made between the MNF and individual civilian providers, rather than the national government acting as a guarantor of support.

(2) **Organization.** The allies or coalition partners normally are expected to provide all the personnel and equipment required to conduct their portion of the NEO. Further, nations may be required to transfer some level of authority over their national logistic force contributions at an agreed time for a specified period. In an extensive NEO, the MNFC may establish a multinational logistic command, which may consist of an operational element and a multinational joint logistic center, as its core.

h. **Terminology.** When planning a multinational NEO, some differences in terminology used by the alliance or coalition nations and that used in this publication will become evident. Annex I, NATO/National NEO Terminology, of AJP-3.4.2, *Allied Joint Doctrine for Noncombatant Evacuation Operations,* provides some examples.

CHAPTER III
COMMAND AND CONTROL

"Your greatness does not depend upon the size of your command, but on the manner in which you exercise it."

Marshal Ferdinand Foch

1. Introduction

a. The US ambassador, with the approval of the Under Secretary of State for Management, can authorize the ordered or authorized departure of USG personnel and dependents other than uniformed personnel of the Armed Forces of the United States and designated emergency-essential DOD civilians who are not under the authority of the US ambassador. While the ambassador cannot order the departure of private US citizens and designated other persons, the ambassador can offer them USG evacuation assistance. Normally an evacuation starts IAW the embassy's EAP, using scheduled airlines, chartered flights, or surface transportation.

b. Military assistance is provided in a variety of circumstances, not just when requirements exceed the capability of the diplomatic mission. When SECSTATE requests military assistance from DOD, approval and the military response are directed by the President or SecDef through CJCS to the appropriate GCC, who will initiate military operations. When hostilities or disturbances occur with complete surprise or appear imminent, the ambassador may invoke such elements of the EAP as the situation warrants, including requesting assistance of the appropriate military commander, while simultaneously informing DOS.

c. The President should be advised as appropriate by SecDef (or a designated representative) when forces are pre-positioned to support a possible evacuation, before the execution of a NEO, and as necessary, thereafter.

2. Command Relationships

a. Within the country, the ambassador has been designated as the responsible authority for the operation. Subject to the overall authority of the ambassador, responsibility for the conduct of military operations in support of an evacuation and security of personnel, equipment, and installations within the designated operational area is vested with the JFC. Figure III-1 depicts the chain of command for a NEO.

b. **Decisions During Planning.** Due to time constraints and the unusual command relationship with respect to NEOs, operational planning and decision making must be based on a foundation of common understanding of perspectives (political and/or military) concerning the situation, mission, objectives, procedures, and free exchange of information. In cases when significant differences between the JFC and ambassador become obstacles to the success of the operation, they are referred to their respective superiors for resolution.

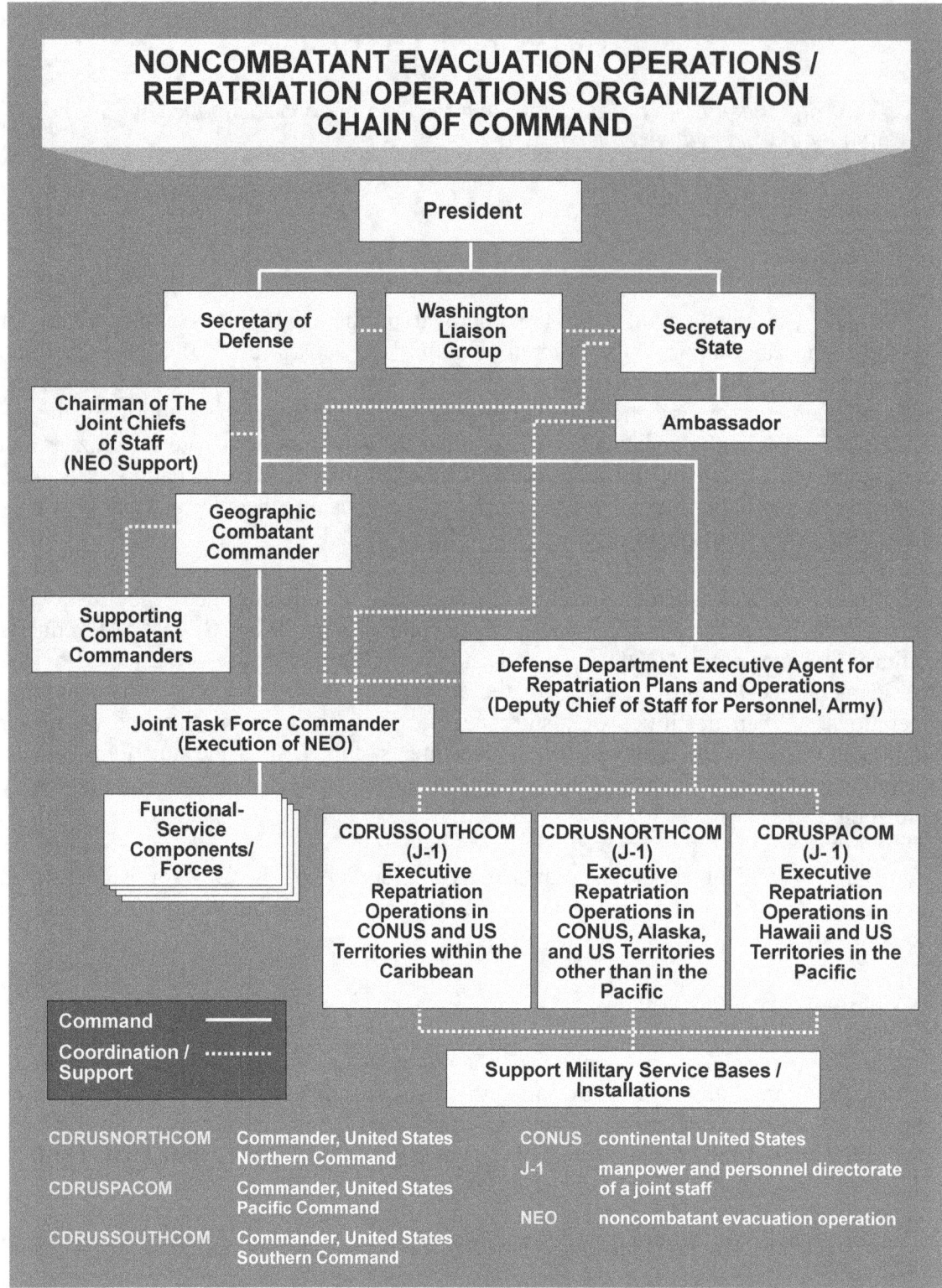

Figure III-1. Noncombatant Evacuation Operations/Repatriation Operations Organization Chain of Command

c. **Consultation Between the Ambassador and JFC.** In the course of planning and executing a NEO, the ambassador obtains and considers the opinions and professional judgment of the JFC. This requirement, however, in no way limits the ambassador's overall responsibility.

d. **Direction to Personnel.** All necessary orders from the ambassador, the GCC, or the JFC to corresponding personnel are, insofar as possible, issued through the appropriate chain of command. In the event communications cannot be established with higher authority or if the situation deteriorates to one of combat operations rather than a NEO (regardless of the environment) and US lives are at risk, the responsible military commander takes whatever action is necessary to protect the lives of US personnel, informs the ambassador of actions taken, and requests guidance through the DOD chain of command.

3. Command and Control

a. Guidance provided by higher authority normally covers areas of key concern to the President and SecDef and provides the supported GCC with an overview of the diplomatic and political context within which the NEO is being considered. The scope and objective of US involvement in a developing situation requiring a military response are often provided in general terms to allow maximum flexibility in the preparation of appropriate COAs. The CJCS warning order defines command relationships, the anticipated mission, and any planning constraints. The warning order also identifies available forces and strategic mobility resources and establishes tentative timing for execution or requests that the GCC develops as part of his COA.

b. **Chairman of the Joint Chiefs of Staff.** CJCS is responsible for the following:

(1) When authorized by SecDef, coordinate the deployment and employment of US forces and equipment in support of the NEO.

(2) Appoint the CJCS representative of the WLG to coordinate the execution of NEO responsibilities.

(3) Monitor the capability and effectiveness of military forces in the protection and evacuation of noncombatants.

(4) Recommend to SecDef transportation movement priorities and USTRANSCOM taskings to provide the appropriate transportation resources in support of DOS requests.

(5) As a member of the WLG, coordinate with DOS, CCDRs, and the Services in the recommended designation of temporary safe havens and ISBs.

(6) When conditions of potential hazard warrant, recommend to the Assistant Secretary of Defense (Force Management and Personnel) that the movement of DOD noncombatants into affected countries be suspended.

(7) Periodically evaluate overseas command procedures for NEOs, particularly during scheduled CJCS exercises.

(8) Develop operational oversight guidance for a GCC's employment of the NTS in a NEO.

(9) Establish a standard procedure for the employment of the NTS in support of a NEO.

c. **Secretary of the Army.** The responsibilities of SECARMY include the following:

(1) Appoint the Army member of the WLG.

(2) Act as the designated DOD executive agent for repatriation planning and operations, and coordinate within DOD and other federal agencies (as well as state and local agencies) in planning for the reception of all noncombatants evacuated to the United States during a NEO.

(3) Establish and operate a JRCC.

(4) Ensure the procedures are in place to meet the needs of DOD noncombatants at safe haven locations.

(5) Ensure that procedures are in place to collect valid personnel data from evacuees during the safe haven period and ensure this data is distributed to other DOD agencies as appropriate.

(6) As specified in the *Joint Plan for DOD Noncombatant Repatriation*, manage all requirements identified in support of DOD noncombatants.

(7) As required, provide support for Army dependents evacuated as noncombatants.

d. **Secretary of the Navy.** The responsibilities of SECNAV are as follows:

(1) Appoint the Navy and Marine Corps members of the WLG.

(2) Provide for the designation and training of port LNOs.

(3) When requested, provide augmentation support to the JRCC, including appropriate Marine Corps and (if OPCON is delegated to the Navy) Coast Guard assets.

(4) As required, provide support for Navy, Marine Corps, and Coast Guard dependents evacuated as noncombatants.

e. **Secretary of the Air Force.** The responsibilities of SECAF are as follows:

(1) Appoint the Air Force member of the WLG.

(2) Provide augmentation support to the JRCC, when requested.

(3) As required, provide support for Air Force dependents evacuated as noncombatants.

> *"Fighting with a large army under your command is nowise different from fighting with a small one: it is merely a question of instituting signs and signals."*
>
> **Sun Tzu**
> **The Art of War**
> **c. 500 BC**

f. **Geographic Combatant Commanders.** The responsibilities for the commanders of geographic combatant commands are as follows:

(1) Prepare and maintain plans for the protection and evacuation of US noncombatants IAW DOS and DOD MOU.

(2) Cooperate with the ambassador and principal officers in the preparation of a consular or the embassy's evacuation plan, contained in the EAP.

(3) Appoint the military members to the RLGs.

(4) Review all DOS EAPs for countries and consular districts in their AOR. If during the review of EAPs any of the criteria are not met, corrective action should be requested via the appropriate ambassador. Criteria to evaluate include the following:

(a) Adequate provisions to protect and evacuate noncombatants.

(b) Accurate references to the use of US military facilities.

(c) Accuracy of specific planning guidance.

(d) Distribution lists for subordinate and adjacent military commands and joint forces.

(e) Procedures for periodic review.

(5) Prepare and maintain plans for the evacuation of military personnel not included in consular and/or embassy plans, and these plans must also identify the emergency-essential civilians who will not be evacuated.

(6) Ensure that plans are prepared for evacuation of military personnel not included in the embassy, staff, and DOD key and emergency essential civilians operating in support of combat units who will be evacuated after the NEO is executed.

(7) When conditions of potential hazard warrant, recommend to SecDef that movement of DOD noncombatants into countries or areas be suspended. Also, recommend evacuation of DOD noncombatants if conditions warrant.

(8) If time precludes adequate communication with DOS or DOD and upon request of the ambassador, provide assistance for the protection and evacuation of noncombatants. If timely communication with the ambassador or the senior DOS representative is not possible, take proper actions necessary to secure the safety of participating personnel as well as other US personnel and foreign nationals who request assistance.

(9) Upon completion of an evacuation involving DOD resources or personnel, provide SecDef with an after action report containing a summary of the activities and recommendations for improving future operations.

(10) Determine lift requirements; if they exceed theater capabilities, coordinate the request for, and the tasking of, airlift and sealift to support the NEO. Lift requirements and AE are requested through USTRANSCOM, where they must be validated prior to action being taken by Air Mobility Command (AMC) or the Military Surface Deployment and Distribution Command.

(11) Maintain geospatial intelligence base for contingency operations (GIBCOs): The GIBCO is a merging of the geospatial-intelligence contingency package and the geospatial-intelligence base mobile visualization tool. GIBCO is an NGA mobile visualization tool on digital video disc (DVD) available through NGA or through the Defense Logistics Agency.

(12) Request assistance from US Special Operations Command Integrated Survey Program and other geographic combatant commands, as appropriate, when requirements exceed the capabilities of the theater personnel.

(13) Designate a JFC, as required.

(14) Arrange for overflight and access agreements within their AORs to support en route activities and provide transportation and other force and asset requirements as requested by the supported GCC.

The successful, safe, and orderly evacuation of noncombatants largely depends on the geographic combatant command's ability to coordinate the operation with the Department of State and supporting commands.

(15) Ensure the required quantities of NTS are on hand, operational, and readily available to support the anticipated volume of evacuees.

(16) Coordinate with DOS and supported embassies to identify support required at evacuation sites and temporary safe havens; in cases where DOS needs assistance, provide contracting support to facilitate life support of evacuees.

g. **US Special Operations Command.** The responsibilities of CDRUSSOCOM are as follows:

(1) Be prepared to provide SOF in support of NEOs conducted by GCCs.

(2) Appoint the SOF representative of the WLG.

(3) Ensure the NTS connectivity requirement during a NEO is addressed in each GCC's SOF communications plan and that satellite communications (SATCOM) connectivity is available at the NEO site.

h. **US Transportation Command.** The responsibilities of the Commander, USTRANSCOM, include providing transportation to meet requirements as requested by the JFC and validated by the supported GCC.

i. **US Strategic Command.** The responsibilities of the Commander, United States Strategic Command (USSTRATCOM), are to function as the single POC for military space operational matters, except as otherwise directed by SecDef. USSTRATCOM's Joint Space Operations Center (JSPOC) serves as the POC for GCCs for military space operational matters. JFCs and their components should request space support early in the NEO planning process to ensure effective and efficient use of space assets. USSTRATCOM provides space force enhancement operations such as weather data, strategic warning, communications, navigation, and intelligence in support of military operations. The JSPOC can also provide necessary coordination for space support from national, civil, and commercial agencies.

4. **Joint Task Force Organization**

a. The supported GCC has the authority to organize forces to best accomplish the assigned mission based on the concept of operations (CONOPS). As such, the supported GCC could decide to assign the NEO mission to a Service component or establish a JTF. If a JTF is formed, it will be established and organized IAW JP 1, *Doctrine for the Armed Forces of the United States*, and JP 3-33, *Joint Task Force Headquarters*. The JFC is responsible for all phases of the operation to include the ISB and temporary safe haven (if located outside the United States and within the joint operations area [JOA]). An ISB or temporary safe haven outside the JTF JOA falls under the responsibility of the supported GCC. The NEO JTF is typically responsible for support and transport of the evacuees to ISBs and safe havens outside the JOA. The JFC exercises OPCON over assigned and attached forces with the authority to organize forces to best accomplish the assigned tasks based on the CONOPS.

OPERATION ASSURED RESPONSE

In 1996, the US military assisted in safeguarding and evacuating Americans from Liberia when that nation's civil war reignited into factional fighting and general violence. During the first week of April 1996, as a result of intense street fighting during the ongoing civil war, about 500 people sought refuge on American Embassy grounds and another 20,000 in a nearby American housing area. On 6 April, the President approved the US ambassador's request for security, resupply, and evacuation support.

Elements of the USS Guam amphibious ready group and the 22nd Marine Expeditionary Unit (Special Operations Capable) [MEU(SOC)], were ordered to the vicinity of Monrovia, Liberia. Upon arrival, the 22nd MEU(SOC) commanding officer assumed command of Joint Task Force-Assured Response (JTF-AR) which included Air Force, Navy, and Marine forces.

Between 9 April and 18 June 1996, JTF-AR evacuated 2,444 people (485 Americans and 1,959 citizens of 68 other countries). Initially, Navy-Marine Corps forces provided embassy security and evacuated 309 noncombatants, including 49 US citizens. The bulk of noncombatants were evacuated by Air Force forces from Special Operations Command Europe. On 9 April, less than 72 hours after the decision to deploy US forces, the first MH-53 helicopter landed in Monrovia to begin operations. Air Force KC-135 tankers and C-130 transports were put on alert in Europe to support 24-hour operations, while other mobility aircraft began to deliver critical medical supplies, food, water, fuel, and communications gear.

Those evacuated continued on US helicopters through Freetown, Sierra Leone, then on MC-130s to Dakar, Senegal, all under the cover of AC-130 gun ships. Throughout the rest of the week, the evacuation continued, as well as airlift of critical supplies, to sustain the effort. By 14 April, the evacuation was essentially complete, however, security and sustainment operations continued through 3 August.

While still conducting this operation, elements of JTF-AR were ordered to Bangui, Central African Republic, to conduct similar operations. A special purpose Marine air-ground task force, embarked on the USS Ponce and with 10 days' notice, relieved the USS Guam task force and assumed the duties of Commander, JTF-AR. This was done to allow the Guam ready group and the 22nd MEU(SOC) to return to the Adriatic Sea and provide US European Command's desired over-the-horizon presence during the Bosnian national elections.

SOURCE: GlobalSecurity.org

b. **Composition.** The JTF's composition is delineated in the establishing directive. The JFC exercises OPCON over assigned forces and normally over attached forces through designated component commanders. Other forces may operate in support of or under tactical control of the JFC, as directed by the GCC.

   c. **Joint Task Force Headquarters Organization.** The JFC organizes the JTF staff. The JTF HQ composition, location, and facilities may have a major influence on what the JFC and staff can accomplish. An afloat JTF HQ may have limitations that could affect staffing levels and equipment capabilities. A JTF HQ located in a neighboring country may not have restrictions on space or amount of equipment. However, such a JTF HQ may encounter restrictions resulting from increased distances, political sensitivities (of the neighboring country), and other types of limitations.

Intentionally Blank

CHAPTER IV
CONTINGENCY AND PREDEPLOYMENT PLANNING CONSIDERATIONS

> *"The essential thing is action. Action has three stages: the decision born of thought, the order or preparation for execution, and the execution itself. All three stages are governed by the will. The will is rooted in character, and for the man of action character is of more critical importance than intellect. Intellect without will is worthless, will without intellect is dangerous."*
>
> **Hans von Seekt**
> ***Thoughts of a Soldier***

1. United States Embassy and Consulate Plans

a. **Emergency Action Plans.** US embassies and consulates are required to have EAPs for the area under their cognizance. The ambassador is responsible for the preparation and maintenance of EAPs, one section of which addresses the military evacuation of US citizens and designated foreign nationals. The GCC is responsible for reviewing and commenting on EAPs. EAPs are not tactical OPLANs in the sense that military planners think of, but they are the reference materials that support the formulation of an OPLAN. The GCC should review the adequacy of the EAP to support military operations. A copy of the current EAP should be on file and maintained at the appropriate GCC's HQ. EAPs include, but are not limited to, the information shown in Figure IV-1.

b. **Emergency Planning Handbook.** The DOS *Emergency Planning Handbook* (EPH), Volume 12, Foreign Affairs Handbook-1 (12 FAH-1) is a consolidated source of guidance for foreign service posts for planning and dealing with certain emergency situations. The EPH serves as the principal reference for posts in preparing and revising the EAP. Every foreign service post is required to have an operative EPH designed to provide procedures to deal with foreseeable contingencies. This handbook provides a detailed agenda to be addressed by the ambassador and the emergency team for planning an evacuation operation. It also provides a two-page checklist of questions (Military Implementation Checklist) most often asked by military commanders and planners concerning an impending evacuation operation. Appendix D, "Sample Emergency Action Plan Checklists," provides an example of a checklist for a US military assisted evacuation.

2. Military Planning—Combatant Command Plans

Predeployment planning begins when the subordinate JFC receives the warning order from the GCC and lasts until the evacuation force deploys to either an ISB or the evacuation site. Prior coordination with the staffs of the GCC and embassy can significantly improve planning for the JFC. The GCC and staff can provide the JFC with information to begin planning, such as the general OPLANs. See Appendix C, "Noncombatant Evacuation Operations Planning Considerations."

CONTENTS OF EMERGENCY ACTION PLANS

■ Possible courses of action for different threat environments

■ Location of evacuation sites (landing zones, ports, beaches)

■ Anticipated number of evacuees (total number by area) categorized by medical status:

● Persons not requiring medical assistance

● Persons requiring medical assistance prior to evacuation

● Persons requiring medical assistance prior to and during evacuation

● Persons requiring emergency medical evacuation

■ Location of assembly areas and major supply routes

■ Location of command posts

■ Key personnel (name, location, and desired means of contacting them)

■ Description of the embassy communications system, transportation fleet, and warden system

■ Quantity of class I (subsistence) supplies on hand at the embassy

■ Quantity of class III (fuel)

■ Availability of class VIII (medical supplies)

■ Standard map products of the local area, with annotations identifying critical landmarks

Figure IV-1. Contents of Emergency Action Plans

3. Intelligence Sources

a. GIBCOs contain specific maps, charts, imagery, and other geospatial products to support evacuation planning and operations. GIBCOs are replacing the NEO package for each country, city, or region. The NGA produces GIBCOs, which give users flexibility through the use of Web browser technology for navigation and display of geospatial data. Applications of the GIBCO are broad, including the capability to become familiar with a foreign environment; develop a battle scene; plan, coordinate, and execute noncombatant evacuations, contingency operations, urban area missions, and search and rescue operations; as a desk-side reference; and as a means of access to geospatial data and navigation aids where networks or infrastructure have been damaged or do not exist. Tailored to each customer's request, each DVD can hold an entire country or an intensified coverage down to a single facility.

b. The Defense Intelligence Agency maintains various databases that provide details on diplomatic facilities and associated areas for use in evacuation planning and execution.

c. The Marine Corps Intelligence Activity produces joint expeditionary support products containing maps, charts, imagery, points of entry, and route studies for use during expeditionary operations including evacuation planning and execution.

d. USTRANSCOM maintains the port and airfield collaborative environment Web site, which provides detailed overviews of ports and strategic airfields (capable of C-130s and above) worldwide.

e. Each GCC's joint intelligence operations center (JIOC) maintains Web sites and databases that provide varying degrees of intelligence support for particular countries.

f. During a crisis, the most current situational information available would be found on the DOS Web site (www.state.gov) for the country of interest. If a special link to the evacuation has not yet been established, click on A-Z country pages, then click on the alphabet of the country.

g. Basic information and maps of all of the countries of the world are available in the Central Intelligence Agency home page at www.cia.gov (link to country of interest via the Factbook).

Emergency action plans vary considerably, depending upon the embassy's physical characteristics, its proximity to populated areas, and its security configuration.

h. Additionally, combat support agencies may deploy personnel as part of a national intelligence support team (NIST) to work with the NEO, consistent with other military operations.

For additional information on a NIST, see JP 2-0, Joint Intelligence.

4. Notification Procedures

a. To develop a realistic evacuation plan, the JTF staff should know how long it will take to assemble the evacuees once the decision to evacuate has been made. Communications with potential evacuees may be via a **warden system,** which is a notification system used to communicate to the US population through wardens using telephones, faxes, e-mails, and direct personal contact. A warden coordinator prepares lists of wardens and other contacts to cover areas of assigned responsibilities. The wardens prepare, update, and maintain a list of phone numbers and addresses of US citizens residing in their assigned areas. During an evacuation, each warden receives and distributes messages, keeping individuals informed about the evacuation, and other relevant information.

b. **Shortwave Radio and Commercial Telephone.** Frequently, US citizens and foreign nationals reside outside the large population centers (for example, capitals, large cities, and military bases). Embassy contact with these individuals is often restricted to shortwave radio and commercial telephone systems, which are seldom secure. Shortwave radio and commercial telephone should be used to notify these individuals only if better means are not available. However, only the minimum unclassified information necessary should be transmitted. Significant delays can occur in notifying these citizens that an evacuation has been ordered. This can result in one group of evacuees being at the assembly area while another has yet to be notified of the evacuation.

c. **Recall.** In some cases, a recall system for embassy or consulate personnel is a citizens' band radio system tied to a telephone recall. It is usually fast, reliable, and efficient.

d. **Runners.** In the event of a severe communications outage, personnel acting as runners may be the only way to pass information.

5. Notification Phases

a. Understanding the phases in which potential evacuees are notified is essential in developing a sensible evacuation plan. Figure IV-2 delineates typical notification phases.

b. **Drawdown.** The basic options for drawdown are authorized departure and ordered departure. Departure may be authorized or ordered when it is of national interest to require the departure of some or all employees and/or their eligible family members, or if there is imminent danger to the life of the employee or the lives of the immediate family of the employee. When a drawdown is necessary to protect the lives of US citizens, the COM may act on his or her own authority. In all other circumstances, however, prior approval from

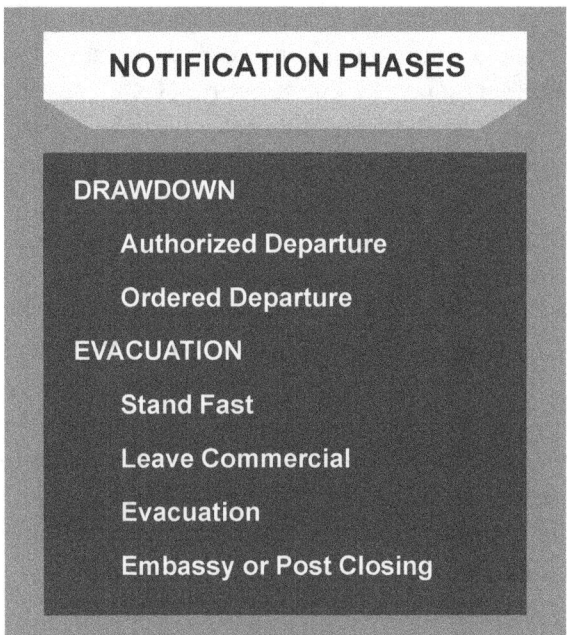

Figure IV-2. Notification Phases

DOS must be obtained. The embassy, referred to as the post, is required to prepare lists of personnel to remain at the post in an emergency situation. The list of employees to remain will include those needed to manage an eventual evacuation of US citizens.

(1) **Authorized Departure.** The ambassador must request authorized departure status from DOS. Employees who wish to leave the post must obtain approval from the ambassador. Family members who wish to leave the post as an official evacuee must also obtain approval from the ambassador. Family members who wish to leave the post not as an official evacuee may do so at any time. When the authorized departure status is terminated, the official evacuees must return to the post.

(2) **Ordered Departure.** The ambassador may determine that a situation has deteriorated to a point that family members and certain employees should leave the post for their safety. Ordered departure is not optional; family members and employees will be issued orders to leave. When the ordered departure status is terminated, official evacuees must return to the post.

c. **Evacuation.** The decision to evacuate personnel assumes that the decision to draw down, at least in part, has been made. When feasible, notification of potential evacuees involves communicating via the established warden system. As a rule, written messages are more reliable than oral messages and should be used whenever possible. There are four notification phases for an evacuation.

(1) **Stand Fast.** When a country's political or security environment has deteriorated and it is perceived that US citizens are threatened, but an evacuation is either not required or is temporarily impossible, all US citizens are requested to "stand fast" and are given preliminary instructions for preparing to evacuate the country. The embassy identifies

the wardens and activates its emergency action organization. The embassy's personnel review the evacuation plans, options, and support requirements, and the ambassador may consider requesting military assistance. The supported GCC may direct the deployment of a liaison team, activate crisis action response teams, and assign a subordinate JFC as appropriate. For a sample stand fast notice, see Appendix E, "Sample Notice Forms."

(2) **Leave Commercial.** Due to the gravity of the situation, nonessential US citizens may be told to leave by commercial transportation as soon as possible. If commercial transport will not be available or adequate, the US embassy may coordinate for increased commercial flights or contract flights to assist US citizens departing voluntarily. The following other actions may take place. The embassy's internal security force may be reinforced by additional MSGs and/or DOS security personnel, or a JTF may be formed to assist in the evacuation. The ambassador might request the deployment of a small JTF liaison team to the embassy to assist in evacuation planning and in anticipation of the requirement for military assistance to conduct the evacuation. For a sample leave commercial notice, see Appendix E, "Sample Notice Forms."

(3) **Evacuation.** When the political or security environment is believed to have deteriorated to the point that the safety of US citizens is threatened, the ambassador (with DOS approval) orders the departure of the personnel listed below in subparagraph 6c, "Personnel Eligible for Evacuation Assistance," keeping only essential personnel of the country team. The embassy would assemble, document, and begin assisting in the movement of US citizens, HN nationals, and TCNs to designated safe haven sites. Of note is per the DOS 12 FAH-1, *Emergency Planning Handbook,* safe haven in the United States is not available for either TCNs or foreign service nationals. Requests for exceptions will be sent to SECSTATE for a decision. A mix of commercial charter, private, or military transport might be necessary, depending on the availability of scheduled commercial transportation. At some point in this phase, the ambassador might request military assistance, either because the transportation means are inadequate or because of the severity of the threat to the evacuees. Once requested, the supported GCC, upon direction from SecDef through CJCS, commences military evacuation operations. These may range from simple transportation support to the deployment of a JTF. A sample evacuation notice is provided in Appendix E, "Sample Notice Forms."

(4) **Embassy or Post Closing.** The situation may deteriorate to the point that the embassy must close and all remaining US citizens and embassy employees must be evacuated. This will not include private US citizens and their dependents who desire to remain in the country. A list of personnel who cannot be ordered to depart a country is provided below in subparagraph 6c, "Personnel Eligible for Evacuation Assistance." Military assistance might not be required until this phase of the evacuation. JTF operations could range from removing the remainder of the country team to full-scale evacuation operations. A sample embassy or post closing notice is provided in Appendix E, "Sample Notice Forms."

6. Evacuee Identification

a. The first question most often asked by both diplomatic and military planners is, "Who are the evacuees, and how many of them will there be in a crisis?" There are several groups of evacuees, some of whom the ambassador may direct to evacuate and some whom the ambassador cannot. Understanding how evacuees are organized, notified, and moved to assembly areas helps in determining the number of potential evacuees and assembly time estimates.

b. **Report of Potential Evacuees.** The report of potential evacuees, also known as the F-77 Report, identifies the numbers of potential evacuees at each embassy. Each embassy or consulate is required to submit to DOS an annual report, on 15 December, of the estimated number of potential evacuees in its assigned area. A copy of the most recent report must be filed with the EAP. F-77 Reports are available on the SECRET Internet Protocol Router Network (SIPRNET) at http://ses.state.sgov.gov/f77/.

(1) The accuracy of the report depends on the general level of interest in the potential for an evacuation. The fear that an evacuation may be required is often the most powerful motivator to get an accurate evacuee estimate.

(2) These counts, however, are only yearly estimates. The accuracy of the estimate will vary with the speed and severity of the crisis. If the whole population of a country suddenly perceives a deadly threat, evacuee numbers and panic will be abnormally high. Evacuee estimates will probably be fairly accurate if the period preceding the evacuation has allowed for an orderly assembly of people who want to get out and the perceived threat at the time of the evacuation remains relatively constant. Note, too, that the estimate may be high or low due to seasonally dependent tourism.

c. **Personnel Eligible for Evacuation Assistance**

(1) The following prioritized categories of personnel are eligible for evacuation assistance and can be ordered to depart.

(a) US civilian employees of all USG agencies (except DOD employees of military commands who have been designated as emergency essential).

(b) US military personnel assigned to the embassy (e.g., DAO, security assistance personnel, MSGs).

(c) Peace Corps volunteers.

(d) US citizens employed on contract to a USG agency if the contract so provides.

(e) Legal and authorized family members of those above.

(f) Family members of all other US military personnel (command-sponsored dependent and noncommand sponsored).

(2) The following categories of personnel are entitled to evacuation assistance, but cannot be ordered to depart. If these individuals refuse to evacuate, the JTF marshalling team should obtain their signature on the Waiver of Evacuation Opportunity (see Figure E-5), which should be forwarded to the embassy. If they depart the country, they may return at their discretion and at their expense. These personnel are as follows:

(a) US citizens employed by non-USG organizations (e.g., World Health Organization).

(b) US citizens employed by or assigned to IGOs and NGOs (e.g., United Nations [UN] Disaster Relief Coordinator, UN High Commissioner for Refugees, International Medical Corps).

(c) US citizens employed on contract directly by the host government, even though the contract may be funded by the USG.

(d) US citizens employed by private entities, such as relief organizations, even though the employer may receive some USG funding.

(e) Fulbright grantees and US citizens in comparable roles.

(f) Other private US citizens.

(g) Family members of private US citizens, to include alien spouses, children, and other bona fide residents of the household.

(3) The category of non-US citizens seeking assistance can be the largest and most difficult to control during a fast-moving evacuation in an uncertain or hostile environment. The ambassador should establish the policy identifying who will receive evacuation assistance. While the United States does not have agreements that guarantee evacuation assistance to any nation, DOS can grant evacuation assistance to citizens from third countries following the initiation of an evacuation. Also, planners should keep in mind that facilities to process US citizens will become overwhelmed if the points of departure do not have the required processing facilities to handle non-US citizens and the volume of people a NEO can create. To the maximum degree possible, NEOs that include non-US citizens should be conducted with commercial aircraft delivering to major commercial international airports. When military airfields/military aircraft are used and non-US citizens are a part of the evacuation, initiate reception planning with DOS and the HN if another country is designated as a safe haven, or if evacuating to the US, DHS should be notified as far in advance as possible.

7. Coordination With Senior In-Country Military Officials

a. The JFC should establish and maintain close liaison with the SDO, who is usually the DATT or the SAO. The SDO will be able to assist in the coordination of JTF activities with the embassy and to assist the JFC in obtaining the ambassador's evaluation of the situation. Additionally, the SDO is able to provide information on the general scope of in-country activities for all DOD noncombatant command elements, including missions, locations, organizations, and unique security requirements.

b. As part of the planning process, the JFC prepares a commander's estimate covering the various options deemed feasible and any pros and cons relating to each, including political constraints. The CJCS or GCC warning order will normally provide the JFC with a concise statement of the US national interests at stake in the NEO, to include:

    (1) The safety and welfare of US citizens.

    (2) The continued stability of the local government.

    (3) The maintenance of a firm posture against terrorism.

    (4) A demonstration of support for international commitments.

    (5) The probable environment in which the NEO will be conducted.

c. The ambassador should summarize the political objectives and constraints relevant to the JTF's assistance, the nuances involved, and any constraints on the use of force that might be appropriate. While these may be obvious to those intimately involved with the situation, the JFC will be better prepared to comply effectively with a request for help if the reasons have been clearly explained.

8. Embassy Security and Operations

a. Security outside the embassy is the responsibility of the HN, while security of the ambassador and embassy grounds is the responsibility of the RSO. In many cases, US embassies do not have security forces or personnel. If security is provided, the RSO has DOS security personnel and a small MSG detachment to accomplish this mission. During the evacuation, the MSG detachment personnel receive their orders from the RSO, while JTF personnel receive their orders from the JFC. JTF personnel do not receive orders from the RSO. These command relationships can potentially cause problems, especially when MSG personnel and JTF personnel work together during the evacuation operation. It is vital that the JTF staff work out missions and command relationships before the operation. The JFC must understand the ambassador's security plan and integrate the joint forces as smoothly as possible.

b. The embassy evacuation plans may not provide for the embassy site to be a primary assembly area or evacuation site. However, experience shows that during times of crisis large numbers of US citizens, citizens of the HN, and TCNs will go to the US embassy.

These people will be frightened and may want to leave the country, but may not have been included in the notification plan or could not reach the designated assembly area or evacuation site. Separate plans should be developed to deal with these crowds, both as a threat to the embassy and as evacuees.

c. Local citizens wishing to volunteer information may arrive at the embassy perimeter without prior notice. These individuals are called walk-ins. Embassies have standing operating procedures (SOPs) on the treatment of walk-ins designed to ensure quick and secure access to the appropriate embassy officers. JTFs should familiarize themselves with these SOPs.

d. In some cases local contract guards control the perimeter of each embassy. These personnel may or may not be armed. Quality of the local guard force varies by country. Some local guards are professional and staffed with personnel who have proven their loyalty to the embassy's staff. These local guards can be very useful in assisting US forces assigned to perimeter security duty. Planning must consider that some or all local loyal contract guards may desire to be evacuated. Planning for numbers to be evacuated should include this additional group. In addition, in the event these guards desire to be evacuated at the last minute, consideration must be made for replacement security.

e. MSGs control access into critical facilities where classified material is processed and stored. MSGs have reaction plans to defend these facilities and destroy or evacuate sensitive material or equipment, if necessary.

9. **Repatriation Considerations**

a. **General.** Repatriation is the procedure whereby US citizens are officially processed back into the United States following evacuation from overseas. Although repatriation is not part of, but subsequent to a NEO, the information provided below should be understood by the NEO JFC and other key joint force members.

b. **Plans**

(1) **DODD 3025.14,** *Noncombatant Evacuation Operations,* **designates SECARMY as the designated DOD executive agent for repatriation planning and operations.** SECARMY is responsible for repatriation of DOD noncombatants. When requested, the Army shall also provide repatriation services to non-DOD personnel. Consequently, **the Army has developed the** *Joint Plan for DOD Noncombatant Repatriation (Non-Emergency).*

(2) For the role of DHHS in repatriation of evacuees returning to the United States, see Chapter II, "Roles, Coordination, and Interaction," paragraph 4, "Other Agencies," subparagraph b, "Department of Health and Human Services."

(3) All **GCCs** must plan for possible repatriation contingencies.

c. **Coordination**

(1) Commander, **USTRANSCOM, along with the supported GCC and the JRCC**, coordinates the flow of evacuees to ports of debarkation.

(2) The **JRCC** maintains oversight of the entire repatriation operation and keeps DOD and other federal agencies informed about repatriation matters.

d. **Funding.** The **Services and DOD agencies** provide funding for safe haven expenses for their respective evacuees. The Service components have the authority to provide special allowances for their Service members and family members under an authorized or ordered evacuation from an overseas location. Federal employees and their family members are also authorized pay and special allowances. Financial entitlements include, but are not limited to, advance payments (when authorized by sponsor), travel, safe haven allowances, and subsistence expense allowances to authorized individuals, and legal claims settlements when authorized by SecDef and/or parent organization.

e. **Public Affairs.** The **Office of the Assistant SecDef (Public Affairs)** supervises the PA aspects of all repatriation operations and approves the proposed PA guidance submitted by subordinate DOD organizations and commands.

f. **Evacuee Information Documentation**

(1) **Instrument.** Department of Defense (DD) Form 2585, "Repatriation Processing Center Processing Sheet," is the standard form used to document the movement of an evacuee from a foreign country to a designated safe haven. **DD Form 2585 should be provided to the evacuees and completed by them prior to their arrival at the repatriation center.** See Appendix F, "Repatriation Processing Center Processing Sheet."

(2) **Purpose.** DOS uses the information for evacuation management and planning purposes. The American Red Cross requires the data for communication evacuation information to sponsors remaining in theater. USCIS uses the information for tracking foreign nationals evacuated to the United States. DHHS uses it to facilitate delivery of personal and financial services, to recoup those costs and to identify individuals who might arrive with an illness requiring quarantine. Additionally, state and local health departments need and use the information to further implement the quarantine of an ill individual. Finally, DD Form 2585 provides a basic data source for the information recorded in the NTS and the Automated Repatriation Reporting System. Information in these two automated systems is routinely used to inform evacuee's family members of their current location and final destination.

g. **Family Assistance.** DOD family centers provide assistance for DOD and/or non-DOD civilian employees and family members affected by an evacuation from an overseas country throughout the entire safe haven period. These family centers provide essential services during the repatriation operation and follow-on assistance and aid when families reach their final safe haven destinations.

h. **Pets.** Although the evacuation of pets is not authorized by Federal regulations, experience has shown that evacuees will bring their pets; therefore, repatriation centers and intermediate staging/processing locations should be prepared to take care of pets if approved by DOS. Families are financially responsible for moving their pets to and from the theater. Transportation of pets at government expense is not an entitlement. Veterinary assistance for pets should be made available at the repatriation sites as required.

i. **NEO Documents.** GCCs and Service commanders outside the United States should identify the documents an individual would require to assist them in preparing for an evacuation during their initial assignment in-processing. A complete listing and explanation of all suggested NEO packet items, to include all of the documentation required for each evacuee and/or family to receive proper safe haven entitlements and process through the repatriation site expeditiously, may be found in the *Joint Plan for DOD Noncombatant Repatriation (Non-Emergency)*.

CHAPTER V
EMPLOYMENT AND EVACUATION OPERATION PROCEDURES

"A prince or general can best demonstrate his genius by managing [an operation] exactly to suit his objectives and his resources, doing neither too much nor too little."

Carl von Clausewitz

1. Evacuation Plan Implementation

a. While the military may play a key role in planning and conducting the operation, it is most often viewed as the last resort in a series of evacuation options. It is important for the JFC and staff to understand this role when preparing a plan for the evacuation. It might be quite natural to assume that the evacuation is a unilateral military operation and prepare the evacuation plan in a vacuum, ignoring the ambassador's requirements and perspective for the NEO. The military and DOS representatives must therefore conduct extensive coordination to ensure the development of a feasible and supportable military plan that supports the ambassador's requirements and objectives.

b. **Evacuation Site Operations.** Operations at the evacuation site are clearly delineated between those performed by DOS personnel and those performed by the JTF. However, in cases of emergency the JTF should be prepared to perform functions that are normally executed by embassy staff. This includes an awareness of movement plans using commercial and private aircraft, ships, and vehicles and all COAs being considered by the ambassador.

c. **Authority to Invoke.** Once SECSTATE approves an evacuation, the ambassador has the authority to implement the plan in a crisis. DOS, acting on the advice of the ambassador, will determine when US citizens and foreign nationals are to be evacuated. When unexpected violence flares up or appears imminent and communications with DOS are cut off, the ambassador may invoke such elements of the plan and initiate such actions as the situation warrants.

2. Advance Party

a. As early as possible in the planning, the JFC forms the advance party and requests permission to send it to the site of the operation. The advance party may consist of two elements: the FCE and the evacuation site party. In a permissive or uncertain environment, the FCE should be inserted before any evacuation site parties. In a hostile environment, the ambassador's decision will probably be to insert the entire evacuation force to immediately commence the operation. **The FCE coordinates with in-country DOS personnel and HN authorities (when authorized by DOS) and establishes a communication link among the JFC, supported GCC, and DOS. Additionally, the supported GCC may want direct representation with the ambassador during a NEO. The evacuation site party conducts reconnaissance to determine and establish assembly areas and evacuation sites.** If the

JFC elects not to deploy an evacuation site party, the FCE is responsible for performing all of the responsibilities normally assigned to the evacuation site party.

b. **Preparation and Planning.** Deployment of the advance party depends on the mission, enemy, terrain and weather, troops and support available, time available, and political considerations. The least conspicuous method is for the advance party to arrive in the HN in civilian clothes on civilian aircraft. This is possible only if the necessary passport and visa arrangements can be made and the environment is permissive. An uncertain or hostile environment may require forcible entry. Use of military aircraft allows the advance party to carry additional equipment that may be needed in setting up the evacuation site and establishing communication and liaison. The following advance party tasks should be accomplished during this phase:

(1) Request permission from the ambassador for the advance party to enter the country. The number of FCE members allowed and the insertion method should be requested.

(2) Deploy as soon as possible, and in advance of the main body, to allow maximum time for coordination and to determine external support requirements.

(3) Develop and brief a communication plan for the advance party.

(4) Acquire and review appropriate maps.

(5) Review the embassy's EAP and the EAP checklists, examples of which are provided in Appendix D, "Sample Emergency Action Plan Checklists."

(6) Assemble and inspect required equipment.

(7) Develop and brief a PR plan for the advance party.

(8) Obtain visitor visas for all members of the advance party.

(9) Due to possible sensitivity of the political situation in the HN, determine whether the advance party should deploy in civilian clothes.

(10) Consider weapon and ammunition requirements based on the threat assessment and limitations imposed by the ambassador (COM).

(11) Examine the need for specialized equipment; for example, ordnance to assist DOS officials in destruction of classified equipment and documents or sufficient SATCOM systems to establish communications with the JTF or combatant command HQ.

(12) Determine the medical requirements.

(13) Identify translator and linguistic requirements.

(14) In coordination with the embassy, request overflight and landing rights for appropriate countries IAW DOD 4500.54-G, *Department of Defense Foreign Clearance Guide*.

(15) Review all available intelligence on the proposed NEO; obtain assistance to create requests for information to fill gaps created by missing data.

(16) Assess news media interest in the situation and activities of the JTF and its involvement in the evacuation.

(17) Develop location/staging area to segregate medical evacuees from general evacuees if practical.

c. **Forward Command Element.** The FCE coordinates with the ambassador and members of the country team for information and assistance. The FCE normally submits situation reports (SITREPs) to the JFC. When the main body enters the country, the FCE rejoins the evacuation force and continues operations with the JTF HQ.

d. **Forward Command Element Composition.** The JFC in coordination with the ambassador or his designated representative determines the size and composition of the FCE. The FCE may include the following personnel:

(1) **Officer in Charge (OIC).** Provides direct liaison with the senior DOS official at the embassy to ensure orders of the JFC and the desires of DOS are accomplished.

(2) **Intelligence Officer**

(a) Provides a conduit for intelligence directly from the embassy and evacuation sites.

(b) Coordinates with the DAO, COS, and RSO to provide the evacuation force updated intelligence estimates. The DAO can facilitate access to the daily embassy SITREPs and other intelligence.

(c) Obtains information and intelligence products, including GIBCOs to satisfy JTF intelligence requirements from the country team and other embassy sources.

(d) Considers the following when conducting joint intelligence preparation of the operational environment and developing priority intelligence requirements and other intelligence requirements:

1. Climatological, tidal, astronomical, and lunar phase data.

2. Assets, characteristics, capabilities of ports, airfields, beaches, helicopter landing zones (HLZs), drop zones (DZs), and key facilities of the HN government for communications, utilities, and health services.

3. Identification of hostile and potentially hostile forces and threat systems, including local government forces, rebel groups, dissident forces, student groups, and unorganized mob action, with the focus on their location and potential to become organized.

4. Identification of any third parties (i.e., external countries) that may attempt to hinder evacuation operations.

5. Identification of friendly third parties that could assist the NEO.

6. Potential for hostile infiltration of evacuees.

7. Imagery and other NGA products of required areas (if available).

8. Liaison with intelligence representatives of other US, third country, and HN agencies as appropriate.

9. Need for linguists to assist with debriefings or conduct liaison with foreign nationals as required.

(e) Provide pertinent medical intelligence in support of the NEO to medical staff.

(3) **Operations Officer**

(a) Briefs DOS representatives on the capabilities of the advance party and the JTF.

(b) Answers operational questions concerning the evacuation plan. Briefs the OIC concerning any information the embassy presents that may affect the evacuation plan.

(c) Ensures that support is provided to manifest noncombatant evacuees using the DOD NTS.

(d) Assesses the requirement for deployment of combat forces.

(e) Defines and identifies strategic and/or theater lift requirements.

(f) Coordinates pet policy with DOS representative so veterinary support can be planned, if required.

(4) **Logistics Officer**

(a) Coordinates HN transportation assets needed by the advance party and JTF.

(b) Arranges for supplies the JTF needs but cannot bring (such as water, fuel, medical supplies, and rations).

(c) Coordinates nonorganic JTF heavy equipment and materials handling equipment support.

(d) Provides on-site logistic assistance to facilitate the evacuation.

(e) Coordinates and/or executes contractual HNS agreements.

(f) Reviews strategic and/or theater lift requests for logistic constraints and feasibility.

(5) **Security Officer**

(a) Coordinates with the SDO, RSO, PSO, and/or MSG on security matters.

(b) Determines and advises the OIC on security requirements before and during the NEO.

(6) **Communications Detachment**

(a) Sets up and operates necessary communications equipment.

(b) Determines areas of compatibility between military and DOD and/or DOS on-site communications equipment.

(c) Resolves any frequency problems that may occur.

(d) Determines if HN communications equipment is similar to, or compatible with, US equipment.

(e) Ensures that required single-channel communications equipment is planned for and deployed (high frequency, very high frequency, ultrahigh frequency, and SATCOM). Ensures the NTS airtime requirement is identified in the SATCOM communications plan.

(f) Develops an understanding of the operation of the HN's phone system. Existing domestic telephone lines can be used to back up the military communication systems. Although telephone lines are not secure, manual encryption devices may be used to pass classified traffic and should be planned for. Telephone lines may be the most reliable form of communication, especially to remote evacuation sites. Communications personnel should verify the serviceability of these lines, record numbers, and ascertain dialing procedures for possible use during execution of the NEO.

(g) Establishes reliable and redundant communication links and procedures among the diplomatic mission, supported GCC, and JFC. Communications must be established between the embassy and JFC so diplomatic and politically sensitive situations can be controlled.

(h) Identifies sensitive equipment and/or material that will need to be evacuated or destroyed.

(7) **Medical Team**

(a) Advises the OIC of medical considerations that affect the NEO, to include recommendations for emergent and urgent patient movement (PM) (casualty evacuation medical evacuation [MEDEVAC], AE, etc.)/transport.

(b) Provides immediate medical assistance as required.

(c) Determines characteristics of the evacuation area that are related to the cause and spread of disease; such as terrain, soil, climate, animals, plants, sanitary standards of the native population, and endemic and epidemic diseases present.

(d) Determines the need for special preventive medicine units.

(e) If authorized by the embassy, determines veterinary requirements to prepare pets for movement.

(8) **Air Support Coordinator**

(a) Coordinates both fixed- and rotary-wing aircraft support.

(b) Determines air traffic control requirements.

(c) Provides advice concerning the number and type of air assets required, the technical aspects of HLZs and DZs (including the type of security required), fixed-wing landing strips, and air evacuation routes.

(d) Selects landing zones (LZs).

(e) Provides interface for air-to-ground operations.

(f) Surveys air facilities for possible use to support follow-on forces for conduct of defensive combat operations.

(9) **Air and Naval Gunfire Liaison Officer and/or Fire Support Officer**

(a) Identifies and confirms prospective targets to support the NEO (uncertain and/or hostile environments).

(b) Coordinates targets with appropriate embassy personnel.

(c) Provides initial terminal guidance support and supporting arms control as required.

(10) **Public Affairs Officer**

(a) Advises and assists the OIC on matters concerning the news media.

(b) Serves as a liaison between the OIC and ambassador for PA.

(c) Works with the embassy PAO to publicize evacuation efforts in an effort to generate confidence in and a positive perception of the operation. This is always accomplished in close coordination with the embassy's staff and within the guidelines of approved DOD PA policy.

(d) Provides clear, concise, and timely information through the combatant command PA staff to senior DOD PA agencies. Provides information to the PAOs at the safe havens concerning media opportunities prior to the arrival of evacuees.

(e) Provides security review of media products to ensure that operations security (OPSEC) is not compromised.

(f) Establishes an effective command information program.

(11) **Information Operations (IO) Officer**

(a) Serves as liaison between the OIC and the supporting IO organization commanders/OICs.

(b) Coordinates, deconflicts, and synchronizes IO core, supporting, and related capabilities that support the NEO.

(c) Coordinates with the JTF PAO, embassy PAO, and embassy information officer to ensure that themes and messages are congruent.

(d) Validates the IO and military information support operations (MISO) plans.

(e) As required, obtains the ambassador's approval for MISO products and execution of the IO plan. If a hostile environment exists, the approval authority for MISO products and execution is SecDef, unless the approval authority has been delegated to the supported GCC.

(12) **Military Information Support Operations Officer**

(a) Serves as liaison between the OIC and the supporting MISO organization commanders/OICs.

(b) Coordinates and monitor execution of MISO to support the NEO.

(c) Coordinates with the JTF PAO, embassy PAO, and embassy information officer to ensure that themes and messages are congruent.

(d) Validates the MISO plan.

(e) As required, obtains the ambassador's approval for MISO products and execution of the MISO plan. If a hostile environment exists, the approval authority for MISO products and execution is SecDef, unless authority has been delegated to the supported GCC.

(13) **Civil Affairs (CA) Officer**

(a) Conducts an initial civil-military operations (CMO) assessment of the operational area to validate information and assumptions of the CMO estimate and advise the OIC of CMO-related issues affecting the NEO.

(b) Advises the OIC on how to minimize population interference with evacuation operations.

(c) Maintains close liaison with embassy officials to ensure effective interagency coordination and delineation of CA responsibilities and activities.

(d) Assists the JTF in accomplishing its mission by obtaining civil or indigenous support for the NEO.

(e) Assists DOS in the identification of US citizens and others to be evacuated.

(f) Assists embassy personnel in receiving, screening, processing, and debriefing evacuees.

(14) **Legal Advisor**

(a) Advises the OIC on such legal issues as may arise on scene in preparation for and during execution of the NEO.

(b) Assists in preparing instruction packages on ROE, use of force, use of riot control agents (RCAs), applicable SOFAs, HN laws, weapons confiscation, search and seizures, and civilian detention, and conducts legal review of relevant authorities.

(c) Conducts liaison with embassy and local officials on legal issues as required.

(d) Coordinates plan for the processing and adjudication of claims against the United States with appropriate embassy personnel.

(15) **Explosive Ordnance Disposal (EOD) Technician**

(a) Advises the OIC and embassy staff on bomb identification measures.

(b) Inspects the embassy and potential ECC sites.

(16) **Religious Support Team (RST)**

(a) Advises the FCE OIC on religious support requirements of evacuees that may impact the evacuation process.

(b) Advises the FCE OIC on HN religious issues that may impact the evacuation process.

(c) Provides immediate religious support to military personnel, their dependents, and other authorized recipients, as required.

(d) Provides liaison to HN religious leaders and/or government cultural/religious affairs officials for assistance to the evacuation.

(e) Provides liaison to religion-based NGOs for assistance to the evacuation.

e. **Forward Command Element Tasks.** FCE tasks are shown in Figure V-1.

f. **Evacuation Site Party.** The evacuation site party identifies and, where possible, establishes the assembly areas, evacuation sites, and the ECC site. When the evacuation force enters the country and the evacuation commences, the evacuation site party becomes the operations center and/or section of the ECC. Additional information explaining ECC operations can be found in Chapter VI, "Evacuee Processing."

g. **Evacuation Site Party Composition.** The composition of the evacuation site party is determined by the JFC; however, the size may be limited by the ambassador. It may consist of the following personnel:

(1) HQ commandant or OIC.

(2) Operations officer.

(3) Intelligence officer.

(4) Communications and/or electronics officer.

(5) Personnel officer.

(6) Logistics officer.

FORWARD COMMAND ELEMENT TASKS

☑ Initiate liaison with the diplomatic mission:
  ✓ Brief Department of State (DOS) representatives on the capabilities and missions of the advance party and the joint task force (JTF)
  ✓ Establish a forward command post that can be expanded to the JTF headquarters staff

☑ Provide a continuing presence for planning and ensure a complementary role with DOS personnel

☑ Determine whether the operational environment is permissive, uncertain, or hostile

☑ Advise the joint force commander (JFC) regarding the size and composition of forces required. If specified in the initiating directive, determine whether the JTF is appropriate for the mission

☑ Advise the JFC regarding the time, place, and method for the arrival of the evacuation force

☑ Determine existing political and sociological considerations

☑ Determine attitude of the local population

☑ Establish communications between the forward command element and the JFC:
  ✓ Make the communication link to JFC available to the senior DOS representative
  ✓ Maintain continuous communications for exchange of planning and intelligence information

Figure V-1. Forward Command Element Tasks

(7) Security officer.

(8) CA officer.

(9) IO officer.

(10) PA officer.

(11) Legal advisor.

(12) Air support coordinator.

(13) Medical officer.

(14) RST.

(15) Engineer officer.

h. **Evacuation Site Party Tasks**

(1) Plan, organize, and establish the ECC in preparation for the main body.

(2) Provide direct liaison with the chief of the embassy consular office.

(3) Maintain liaison with civilian or HN government agencies involved in the evacuation.

(4) Conduct ground reconnaissance of proposed assembly areas, evacuation sites, beaches, HLZs and/or DZs, airports, and ports; obtain photographs, where possible. To ensure that aircraft configurations are taken into account, the air support coordinator will be fully aware of the requirements of potential pickup and delivery sites.

(a) Recommend and/or confirm assembly areas, evacuation sites, and HLZs and/or DZs. If required to move assembly area operations, coordinate approval with the ambassador.

(b) Prepare initial evacuation site defensive plan and evacuation security requirements.

(c) Plan and coordinate emergency AE operations for evacuees with serious medical problems.

(d) Plan and coordinate operations of assembly areas and evacuation areas with DOS representatives.

(5) Conduct initial preparation of assembly areas and evacuation sites, to include the following:

(a) Clear minor obstacles.

(b) Plan and layout assembly areas and evacuation sites.

(c) Plan and provide for initial terminal guidance at beaches and HLZs and/or DZs.

(6) Collect essential planning information that includes the following:

(a) Assessment of hostage threat.

(b) Number and categories of evacuees.

(c) Medical status of evacuees.

(d) Safe havens (intermediate, temporary, final) determined by DOS.

(e) Political constraints.

(f) Number of HN personnel and TCNs to be evacuated.

(7) Assist DOS personnel with news media.

(8) Establish and maintain communications with the FCE and embassy.

(9) Coordinate additional security requirements the HN police may be able to provide.

(10) During permissive NEOs, coordinate for overflight rights. In uncertain or hostile environments, consider the need for OPSEC and airspace coordination prior to coordinating overflight rights.

(11) Plan and coordinate health care needs of the evacuee population. Determine endemic disease and environmental threats to the population at risk, mission, and operational commander. Plan for the health care needs of evacuees in transit to safe havens in concert with joint, other USG, intergovernmental, and multinational agencies as necessary.

(12) If pet evacuation is authorized by DOS, establish pet storage and care area.

i. **Deployable Joint Task Force Augmentation Cell.** A GCC may elect to stand up a deployable joint task force augmentation cell (DJTFAC), a liaison and augmentation asset that can be deployed in advance of a JTF advance party. The DJTFAC can serve as both the JFC's advance party and the GCC's liaison until the JTF advance party is deployed and operational.

j. **Standing Joint Force Headquarters Core Element (SJFHQ[CE]).** A GCC may utilize a SJFHQ(CE) as an advance party to a JTF. The SJFHQ(CE) provides the CCDR with a trained, standing joint C2 capability to accelerate the formation of a JTF HQ.

For additional information on SJFHQ(CE), refer to JP 3-0, Joint Operations, *and US Joint Forces Command's Web-based* Common Joint Task Force Headquarters Standing Operating Procedure.

3. Joint Task Force Main Body Organization and Missions

a. A JTF "main body" will deploy to conduct the on-scene evacuation process. After insertion of the main body, each element prepares for its part in the operation. As the advance party rejoins the main body, the main body may consist of a HQ, marshalling element, security element, logistic element, and SOF. The size of the main body depends on the number of evacuees, evacuation sites, assembly areas, and the tactical situation. Figure V-2 depicts the JTF main body. Overall, the JTF organization will comply with JP 1, *Doctrine for the Armed Forces of the United States,* and JP 3-33, *Joint Task Force Headquarters*.

b. JTF HQ. The JTF HQ coordinates and directs the evacuation.

(1) **Forward Command Element.** The FCE joins the evacuation force and continues operations with the JTF HQ. Effective liaison with the embassy will be made by the FCE.

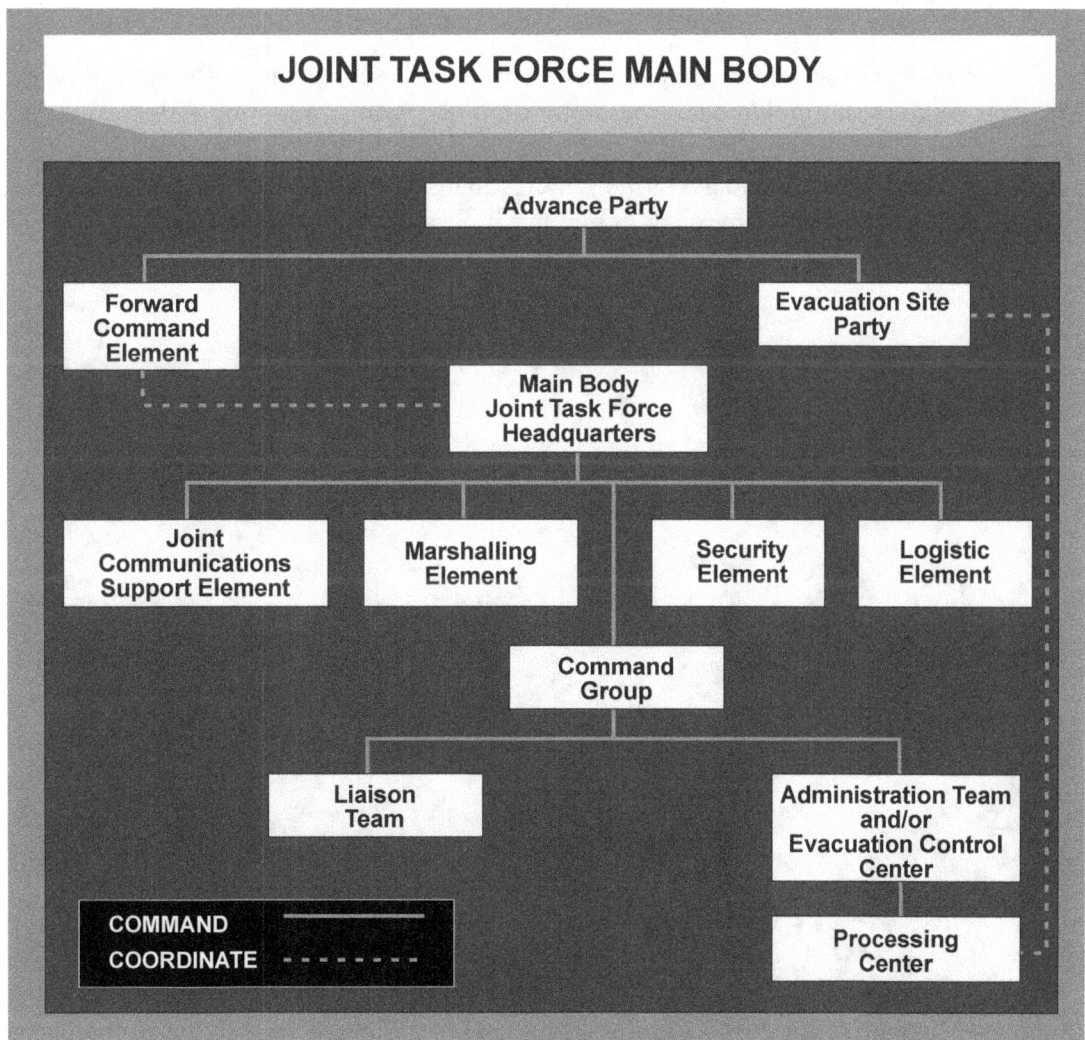

Figure V-2. Joint Task Force Main Body

(2) **Liaison Team.** The liaison activities continue with the embassy, supported GCC, and other agencies as required.

(3) **Administrative Team.** The administrative team joins the evacuation site party to form the ECC. The administrative team is responsible for the smooth operation of the ECC processing center. Processing center operations are discussed in Chapter VI, "Evacuee Processing."

c. **Marshalling Element.** The marshalling element moves to and secures predesignated assembly areas, brings evacuees to the assembly areas, and escorts them to the ECC. The size of the marshalling force depends on the number of sites and evacuees.

(1) **Marshalling Team.** One marshalling team controls an assembly area and evacuates the citizens in that area. The marshalling team should be large enough to organize into two sections that consist of search squads and security squads. Search squads may not be needed if the embassy's evacuation plan has been successfully implemented and all evacuees have been notified. If it has been determined that all evacuees have been informed, then search squads should not leave the assembly area except in emergency cases.

(a) The search squads locate evacuees and escort them to the assembly area. Each search squad should have an interpreter and, if possible, a guide. A lost squad in a potentially hostile environment can create significant problems for the evacuation force. Interpreters may be required to assist the search squads in moving from the assembly areas and to locate evacuees who are not at home or whose addresses are incorrect.

In accordance with mission priorities and available assets, noncombatant evacuation operations may use a number of transportation modes, to include small craft sea transportation.

(b) A security squad provides security to the team during movement and in the assembly area.

(c) Planners consider marshalling team C2 requirements. MISO units (both Army and Marine Corps), military police units, military linguists, contract interpreters, and host and partner nation assets are all examples of assets or units that may be able to provide additional capability.

(2) **Marshalling Force Operations.** The marshalling team locates evacuees and moves them to assembly areas and eventually to the ECC. The marshalling team may have several search squads under the control and direction of the team's OIC. The following should be considered during marshalling operations:

(a) Sufficient transportation for the search and/or security squads and evacuees. All evacuees should be prepared to evacuate by helicopter, small boat or craft, and tracked or wheeled vehicles. Other considerations include:

<u>1</u>. The use of local drivers, if available, because of their experience and familiarity with the local road network.

<u>2</u>. Availability of sufficient mechanics for emergency repairs.

<u>3</u>. Briefing of military drivers on the HN traffic laws and customs.

(b) **Movement control** requires:

<u>1</u>. Identification of environmental factors that will hamper movement (e.g., flooding, weather effects on ground lines of communications).

<u>2</u>. Identifying primary and alternate routes and checkpoints.

<u>3</u>. Having local road maps available for each driver.

<u>4</u>. Planning for convoy control and security.

<u>5</u>. Identifying safe houses or areas if vehicles break down or become separated or lost.

<u>6</u>. Ensuring that adequate communications equipment is available for convoys.

(c) **Assembly area operations** include:

<u>1</u>. Establishment of perimeter security, even in a permissive environment.

<u>2</u>. Sufficient transportation available to move evacuees to the ECC. Vehicles belonging to the evacuees may be used to transport personnel to the ECC.

3. Coordination of staggered movement schedules between several assembly areas and the movement schedule of evacuees to the ECC.

(d) **Search squad operations** include:

1. Obtaining a list of potential evacuees from the consular officer.

2. Obtaining copies of the instructions given to each potential evacuee.

3. Having copies of the Waiver of Evacuation Opportunity readily available (see Appendix E, "Sample Notice Forms") for evacuees who refuse to leave.

4. Briefing each evacuee on the baggage limitations set by the embassy, positive identification requirements at the ECC, and restricted items that may not be transported.

5. Recording the name, sex, age, potential medical problems, and citizenship of each evacuee.

6. Escorting evacuees from the vehicle parking area to the ECC (evacuees may drive their vehicles directly to the ECC, and search personnel should note the individual's name and intent).

7. Identifying evacuees not on the list provided by the embassy.

d. **Security Element.** Security forces are used as necessary at the evacuation sites, ECC perimeter, LZs, aircraft, staging and/or parking areas, and landing sites for naval landing craft. Security forces can also provide a reaction force if a marshalling team or other unit encounters difficulty or requires assistance. To determine the size of the security force, consider the following:

(1) Enemy threat to evacuation operations.

(2) Anticipated response of HN police, military forces, and other friendly forces in and around the evacuation objective area.

(3) Crowd control requirements at each site.

(4) Number of evacuees.

(5) Number of marshalling and search teams required to search for evacuees.

(6) Number of evacuation sites.

(7) Size of the ECC.

(8) Transportation available to cover the assigned areas.

(9) Personal security of the ambassador.

(10) Type of resources used to evacuate personnel.

e. **Logistic Element.** The logistic support provided should be limited to the minimum essential support required for the evacuation. Consideration should be given to the following factors in determining requirements for logistic support of the JTF:

(1) Characteristics of the evacuation area.

(a) Resources available:

<u>1.</u> Existing and potential facilities for support to the JTF, such as facilities for the storage and distribution of supplies, transportation means, airfields, fuel points, medical facilities, medical supplies, and other facilities.

<u>2.</u> Food, water, fuel, and consumables.

(b) Climate, weather, and terrain.

(c) Number of evacuees and their needs.

(2) Potential threats to the evacuation.

(a) Adversary and/or potential adversary strength and activity.

(b) Disposition and location.

(3) Strength and composition of the JTF.

(a) Total troop strength.

(b) Composition of the JTF in terms of ground, air, and maritime combat forces, combat support, and combat service support units.

(c) Logistic support capabilities of each component and separate unit.

(4) Time constraints and duration of operation.

(5) Logistic support required by the embassy and evacuees.

(6) Availability and suitability of HNS as an alternative to deploying US military logistic support.

(7) Prearranged HNS and/or inter-Service support agreements as appropriate.

(8) Capabilities and dependability of the HN transportation system to provide rapid evacuation of combat and noncombat casualties.

4. General Considerations

a. **Medical and Dental.** During evacuation operations, it may be difficult to insert and establish the medical support function for the JTF because of time and operational constraints. Comprehensive and detailed casualty and medical support planning should be implemented to cover immediate medical and surgical treatment points. Special units organized for this purpose may save lives and permit a more expeditious evacuation. Depending on the size and scope of the evacuation operation, there may be the potential for large numbers of both military and civilian casualties. The JFC's medical staff should identify tailored medical packages to treat disease and nonbattle injuries, and to identify and mitigate potential environmental health threats.

(1) **Global Patient Movement Requirements Center (GPMRC).** The GPMRC is a joint activity reporting directly to USTRANSCOM. The GPMRC provides medical regulating services, including clinical validation, limited patient in transit visibility, and evacuation requirements planning for intertheater PM and intratheater for CONUS. The GPMRC coordinates with supporting resource providers to identify available assets and communicates transport to bed plans to Service components, or other agencies, to execute the mission.

(2) **Theater Patient Movement Requirements Center (TPMRC).** Both US Pacific Command and US European Command have a permanent TPMRC that manages the validation and regulation of intratheater PM within their respective theaters. The TPMRC is responsible for theater-wide PM (e.g., medical regulating and AE scheduling) and coordinates with theater medical treatment facilities to allocate the proper treatment assets required to support its role. The TPMRC communicates this transport to bed plan to the theater Service transportation component or other agencies responsible for executing the mission. The TPMRC coordinates with the GPMRC for intertheater PM.

(3) **AE** is the movement of patients under medical supervision to and between medical treatment facilities by air transportation. The Air Force is responsible for operating a common-user, fixed-wing AE system. HQ AMC is responsible for serving as the single AE proponent for the Air Force, managing and operating the intertheater and CONUS AE systems. Intratheater AE is a responsibility of the GCC through the TPMRC. USTRANSCOM, through the GPMRC, will task HQ AMC to provide AE forces to airfields in theater, to evacuate casualties between theaters (intertheater), or from a theater of operations to CONUS reception airfields. Further distribution of patients within CONUS will be coordinated by GPMRC in conjunction with the 618th Tanker Airlift Control Center. Intratheater common-user AE will be provided using a combination of theater-assigned AE units and/or deployment of theater-specific AE elements. Refer to JP 4-02, *Health Service Support,* for additional information on AE.

(4) Other considerations for medical staffs planning NEOs include the following:

(a) Experience has shown that the common medical complaints of personnel being evacuated are nausea, dehydration, and diarrhea. Most frequently, sick evacuees will be children.

(b) Particularly effective medical staffs during NEOs include general medical officers, family practitioners, pediatricians, internists, and psychiatrists and/or psychologists. Additionally, there are usually requirements for medical support staff, including physician assistants, nurse practitioners, nurses, medical corpsmen and/or technicians, and public health officers.

(c) Well-established liaison with local hospitals or medical centers and ambulance service is essential.

(d) A separate area close to the disembarkation point should be designated to perform medical assessments, dispense medication, and conduct patient staging.

(e) Medical staff should consider wearing distinctive clothing or markings to aid in identification.

(f) Medical staffs may anticipate medicinal requests that include antibiotics, antidiarrheals, pain relievers, antibacterial creams, eye and ear drops, cough and cold formulas, high blood pressure medications, and insulin.

(g) Special plans and attention to the situation will be required to move and evacuate personnel hospitalized in HN medical facilities.

(h) AE missions may require movement of urgent or priority patients in aircraft not completely filled. Due to patients' severe conditions, the aircraft will normally not be delayed for nonmedical evacuees to be moved to the airfield in order to fill the aircraft to maximum capacity.

(i) Preventive environmental health services are particularly necessary in some locales to minimize acquiring diseases while waiting in relatively unprotected circumstances.

(j) Primary casualty receiving and treatment ships (PCRTSs) may provide medical treatment resources offshore.

(k) Predeployment planning for medical logistics, to include coordination with the most appropriate theater lead agent for medical materiel for the affected theater, is imperative to ensure proper medical supplies and a resupply process.

(5) Veterinary support may be required if DOS allows pet evacuations. Additional considerations may include means of movement, kennel requirements, identification microchips, gaining country quarantine requirements, vaccination requirements, outgoing physical examinations, health certificates, and rabies certificates.

b. **Personnel Recovery.** If the NEO environment becomes uncertain or hostile, the JFC may need to establish a joint PR center to plan and coordinate PR missions. While primarily organized to recover US military or DOD civilians and DOD contractors authorized to accompany the force, authority also may be granted by the President or SecDef to recover other US or foreign nationals who have become isolated during the NEO.

For further guidance on planning, coordinating, supporting, and executing a PR mission, refer to JP 3-50, Personnel Recovery.

c. **Mortuary Affairs.** Mortuary affairs personnel ensure proper and dignified treatment of human remains. The JTF should plan for mortuary affairs for both military personnel and evacuees. Even in a permissive NEO environment, deaths among elderly, critically ill, or newborn evacuees may be encountered. The decision to transport remains is dependent on but not limited to the specifics of the situation, to include the tactical environment, weather, and capacity of receiving ships and aircraft. (Note: PCRTSs are outfitted with limited morgue facilities.) Under no circumstances should remains be transferred before all evacuees have been safely transported.

For guidance and information pertaining to the search, recovery, evacuation, and identification of the dead or temporary burial of remains in theaters of operations, refer to JP 4-06, Mortuary Affairs.

d. **Strategic Communication.** The USG uses strategic communication (SC) to provide top-down guidance relative to using the informational instrument of national power in specific situations. SC-related activities may play a more important role in the NEO if the environment becomes uncertain or hostile. SC is focused USG processes and efforts to understand and engage key audiences to create, strengthen, or preserve conditions favorable to advancing national interests and objectives through the use of coordinated information, themes, messages, and products synchronized with the actions of all instruments of national power. SC's primary communication capabilities are coupled with defense support to public diplomacy (DSPD) and military diplomacy activities to implement a holistic SC effort. The predominant military activities that support SC themes and messages are PA, IO, and DSPD.

(1) **Public Affairs.** The JFC will ensure that accurate and timely release of information about the operation is made to the media to the maximum extent possible consistent with DOD-approved PA guidance, OPSEC, and the safety of personnel involved. Speed of media transmission makes it probable that a worldwide audience will have immediate access to information about the conduct of the operation and its participants. To ensure that the media do not provide intelligence to persons hostile to the operation, the PAO working with embassy personnel needs to manage PA through accurate and timely releases concerning the NEO. During NEOs, the JTF PAO needs to ensure that all PA announcements have been approved by the ambassador or the designated representative. Additional PAO responsibilities include the following:

(a) Advise the JFC on all aspects of PA.

(b) Develop a PA plan that coordinates all public (media and general public) and command (internal) information functions, including publication of JTF bulletins, newsletters, video tapes, Web pages, and press releases.

(c) Review materials prior to public release.

(d) Establish procedures IAW guidance promulgated by higher authority.

(e) As required, obtain appropriate clearances for press releases.

(f) Distribute information pertaining to the JTF and its operations IAW established command security policies.

(g) Serve as liaison and escort for civilian and military information media representatives. In anticipation of, and prior to operations:

<u>1</u>. Ensure that the information plan is updated daily.

<u>2</u>. Determine PA personnel and equipment requirements.

<u>3</u>. Obtain a current list of legitimate media representatives in country to coordinate release of information during a crisis.

(h) Determine and disseminate JFC guidance on the release of public information.

(i) Provide civilian and military media office space, to include press room or news center near the proposed command post, emergency operations center, or ECC.

(j) During operations:

<u>1</u>. Establish a press conference schedule and conduct press briefings.

<u>2</u>. Provide rapid response to press queries.

<u>3</u>. Disseminate a daily JTF information news bulletin.

<u>4</u>. Disseminate news to subordinate units as appropriate.

For further guidance on PA, refer to JP 3-61, Public Affairs.

(2) **Information Operations.** IO are the integrated employment of the core capabilities of electronic warfare (EW), computer network operations, MISO, military deception (MILDEC), and OPSEC, in concert with specified supporting and related capabilities, to influence, disrupt, corrupt, or usurp adversarial human and automated decision making while protecting that of friendly forces. During a NEO, there may not be an

identified adversary, and some of the capabilities listed above may not be appropriate or relevant. However, the fluid situation often present during a NEO and the frequent occurrence of NEOs with other military operations necessitate the coordination of the appropriate capabilities listed above through the joint IO cell. OPSEC cannot be overemphasized, especially in a nonpermissive environment. It greatly contributes to the protection of forces and the personnel being evacuated.

For further guidance on IO, refer to JP 3-13, Information Operations, *JP 3-13.1,* Electronic Warfare.

(a) **Military Information Support Operations.** The purpose of MISO is to induce or reinforce foreign attitudes and behavior favorable to the originator's objectives. MISO can greatly facilitate NEOs in uncertain or hostile environments. MISO efforts and assets can execute programs and disseminate products that induce an attitude and/or behavior of noninterference toward the NEO among the local populace. Prudent employment of MISO can prevent the degeneration of a permissive or uncertain environment into a hostile environment. JFCs should begin MISO planning as early as possible to ensure approval for execution in support of operations. MISO resources and capabilities provide the commander with a means of influencing hostile and potentially hostile personnel (combatant and civilian) through employment of appropriate media and using the appropriate language(s) and symbols and/or terms of reference. If the JFC desires to employ MISO, that decision should be coordinated with the ambassador and appropriate members of the country team. DOS personnel should be able to provide JTF MISO personnel with valuable information about the target audience and any programs similar to MISO they may have been using in preparation for the NEO or the crisis that precipitated the NEO requirement. MISO efforts in support of NEO can produce the following results:

<u>1</u>. Explain the purpose of US actions and manage and counter disinformation, deception, confusion, and rumor.

<u>2</u>. Assist in establishing control of civilian evacuees, the neutral local populace, and other groups in the operational area to minimize casualties and to prevent interference with friendly military operations.

<u>3</u>. Prevent or deter interference by hostile forces or other nations.

<u>4</u>. Provide continuing analysis of political and cultural factors to maximize political and psychological effects of the operation.

<u>5</u>. Exploit withdrawal of US forces while creating positive perceptions of US intent and goodwill.

<u>6</u>. Support PA, MILDEC, and OPSEC, as required

For further guidance on MISO, refer to JP 3-13.2, Military Information Support Operations.

(b) **Military Deception.** Use of MILDEC to support a NEO in a hostile or uncertain environment can help to mislead adversaries as to the strength, readiness, locations, and intended missions of friendly forces. The MILDEC representative to the IO cell is responsible for incorporating/deconflicting actions planned by other IO capabilities into the deception plan.

For further guidance on MILDEC, refer to JP 3-13.4, Military Deception.

(3) **Defense Support to Public Diplomacy.** DSPD can be used to complement PA and IO efforts during a NEO in a hostile or uncertain environment. PA activities should be planned and coordinated with any other DSPD activities to ensure unity of effort and maximum effectiveness. DSPD can entail the use of a military information support team (MIST) to support a US embassy within a HN. The MIST prepares information products, based on the guidance of the country team to communicate country-specific themes and messages. It could also involve the deployment of a joint public affairs support element (JPASE) team to a contingency location where JPASE representatives work out of the US embassy and coordinate military PA activities with embassy goals and objectives. DSPD requires coordination with both the interagency and among DOD components.

e. **Information Sharing.** Generally, the best approach to information sharing with the NGOs and international civilian community is to keep the focus on complete transparency in sharing operational information and developing a shared situational awareness and understanding of the objectives to achieve the mission. However, classified information will only be shared with or released to individuals with the appropriate security clearance and need to know based on policy and guidance pertaining to the specific operation being conducted. Ensure compliance with National Disclosure Policy-1, *National Policy and Procedures for the Disclosure of Classified Military Information to Foreign Governments and International Organizations.*

LEBANON NONCOMBATANT EVACUATION OPERATION (NEO) 2006

The United States began to evacuate some citizens from Lebanon on 16 July 2006. On 17 July, two Marine Corps CH-53E Sea Stallion helicopters aided in the voluntary departure of 42 American citizens from the US Embassy in Beirut, Lebanon. The citizens were flown to Royal Air Force Base Akrotiri in Cyprus. US citizens who were flown out via helicopter were the elderly, those with small children, and those with special medical needs. Sixty more people were airlifted from the US Embassy on July 18. The Department of Defense (DOD) hoped to evacuate approximately 300 people by air per day. Around 200 people were evacuated by air on 19 July. The Orient Queen (a cruise ship charter by DOD to evacuate US citizens) docked in Beirut on 18 July and left the 19th with about 900 people on board for its first round of transporting evacuees. The ship was escorted by the USS Gonzales (DDG 66) and arrived in Cyprus on the 20th.

The US Sailors and Marines from the Iwo Jima Expeditionary Strike Group (ESG) and the 24th Marine Expeditionary Unit (MEU) assisted in the authorized departure of American citizens from Lebanon. In addition to the Iwo Jima Strike Group and USS Gonzales, three more US ships from US European Command also assisted (USS Barry [DDG 52], USS Mount Whitney [LCC 20], and USNS Big Horn [T-AO 198]). The commander of US Naval Forces Central Command indicated that people were evacuated on US Navy ships as well as the chartered cruise ship. On 20 July, 341 Americans were evacuated out of Southern Lebanon, via a bus convoy, and taken to Beirut Harbor to board the Orient Queen for transport. Also on the 20th, a group of US Marines from Interim Marine Corps Security Force (IMCSF) Bahrain arrived in Beirut to provide security for the commercial vessel Orient Queen as it assisted with the voluntary departures of US citizens. The IMCSF coordinated the security aboard the contracted ship and worked to ensure the safe and orderly transport of each passenger who boarded the vessel. The Marine security team, along with the help of Marines from the 24th MEU, also screened passenger luggage prior to loading it on the vessel.

A landing craft utility (LCU) operated by Sailors assisting the 24th MEU landed in Lebanon, 20 July, to begin transporting American citizens who had chosen to depart that country. The LCU deployed from the USS Nashville (LPD 13) and was the first US naval vessel to land in Lebanon in support of the voluntary departure of US civilians. American citizens boarded the LCUs and were transported to USS Nashville in the Eastern Mediterranean Sea. The USS Nashville then transported the Americans to Cyprus where they made further arrangements for follow-on transportation and accommodations. More US Sailors and Marines from the USS Iwo Jima (LHD 7) ESG and the 24th MEU arrived on station 21 July to assist in the authorized departure of American citizens from Lebanon.

On 21 July, the USS Trenton, the USS Whidbey Island, and the contract carrier Rahmah carried around 4,200 American citizens to safety. The Navy ships carried evacuees to Cyprus, and the Rahmah carried roughly 1,400 Americans to Mersin, Turkey. Turkey offered the seaport of Mersin as an overflow area. Once American evacuees arrived in Mersin, they were bussed to nearby Incirlik Air Base, where the Department of State had chartered air lines to transport them back to the United States.

The Defense Logistics Agency assisted with the evacuation effort by immediately shipping 24,000 individual military meals by military air to Cyprus. The agency also provided 2,000 cots and blankets and ensured fuel was available for US military planes and vessels involved in the evacuation.

On 23 July, the total number of Americans evacuated from Lebanon reached 10,000. A total of 3,994 American citizens left Lebanon on the 22nd. Navy and contract ships lifted 1,815 from the embattled country on the 23rd. The USS Whidbey Island transported 792, and the contract carriers Orient Queen and Rahmah took 983 and 933 Americans, respectively, to Cyprus.

US Transportation Command arranged commercial and military aircraft to fly the evacuees. On July 22, two military flights transported 199 Americans to McGuire Air Force Base, N.J. Chartered commercial flights took evacuees to Baltimore-Washington International Thurgood Marshall Airport and Philadelphia International Airport.

On 24 July, 957 US citizens were evacuated from Lebanon to Cyprus aboard the contracted cruise ship Orient Queen, bringing the total to 12,870 since the crisis in Lebanon began 16 July.

On 25 July, the contract vessel Rahmah ended its contract period with the US effort and made its final run from Beirut to Cyprus

On 26 July, a group of 100 US citizens were taken from southern Lebanon to the port city of Tyre by civilian vehicles, and they joined another 110 Americans leaving on a Canadian ship. About 725 Americans left Lebanon aboard the contracted vessels Orient Queen and Vittoria M.

On July 26, the US military performed its final scheduled evacuation of US citizens from Lebanon. The military had evacuated almost 14,000 US citizens from Lebanon. The US Embassy in Beirut estimated that the vast majority of US citizens wishing to leave Lebanon had now been evacuated. The Orient Queen, the contracted vessel Vittoria M, and the Swift, a high-speed vessel manned by US Navy personnel, would continue to make runs into Beirut evacuating American citizens or delivering humanitarian supplies. The USS Nashville, USS Trenton, USS Whidbey Island, USS Mount Whitney, USS Gonzalez, USS Barry, and the Swift—part of the USS Iwo Jima ESG—remained in the region.

Various Sources

Intentionally Blank

CHAPTER VI
EVACUEE PROCESSING

"...there must be a clear-cut, long-term relationship established between operational intentions and administrative resources. Successful administrative planning is dependent on anticipation of requirements."

Montgomery of Alamein
Memoirs, 1958

1. Evacuation Control Center

The ECC supports DOS, which conducts processing, screening, and selected logistic functions associated with emergency evacuation of noncombatants. The JTF should, however, be prepared to perform functions that are DOS responsibilities, if required. Size and composition of the ECC will be determined by the number of evacuees, evacuation environment, and location of the evacuation area. Of primary importance is the nature of the emergency causing the evacuation; it may be natural, political, or military based.

2. Evacuation Control Center Flow Chart

Figure VI-1 contains a recommended ECC flow chart.

3. Evacuee Processing

a. Evacuee processing may take place in country at an air terminal, onboard ship, or at a temporary safe haven site. Regardless of location, a comprehensive plan for reception, accounting, and care of evacuees should be implemented. The primary duties of the commander, JTF (CJTF), include maintaining order at the evacuation site and supporting the ambassador's efforts to care for noncombatant evacuees.

b. **Procedures During Processing.** At an air terminal, port, or beach, the evacuee processing should be located in a building, tent, or other appropriate place to provide shelter and safety to the evacuees. The area should be staffed with security, interpreter, local immigration, embassy, support liaison, and medical personnel. The following procedures should be considered:

(1) Use military police when available.

(2) Use easily recognizable markings on US personnel, vehicles, and equipment.

(3) Disarm evacuees prior to evacuation processing.

(4) Establish a policy concerning responsibility to secure evacuee valuables during processing, to include pets (if allowed).

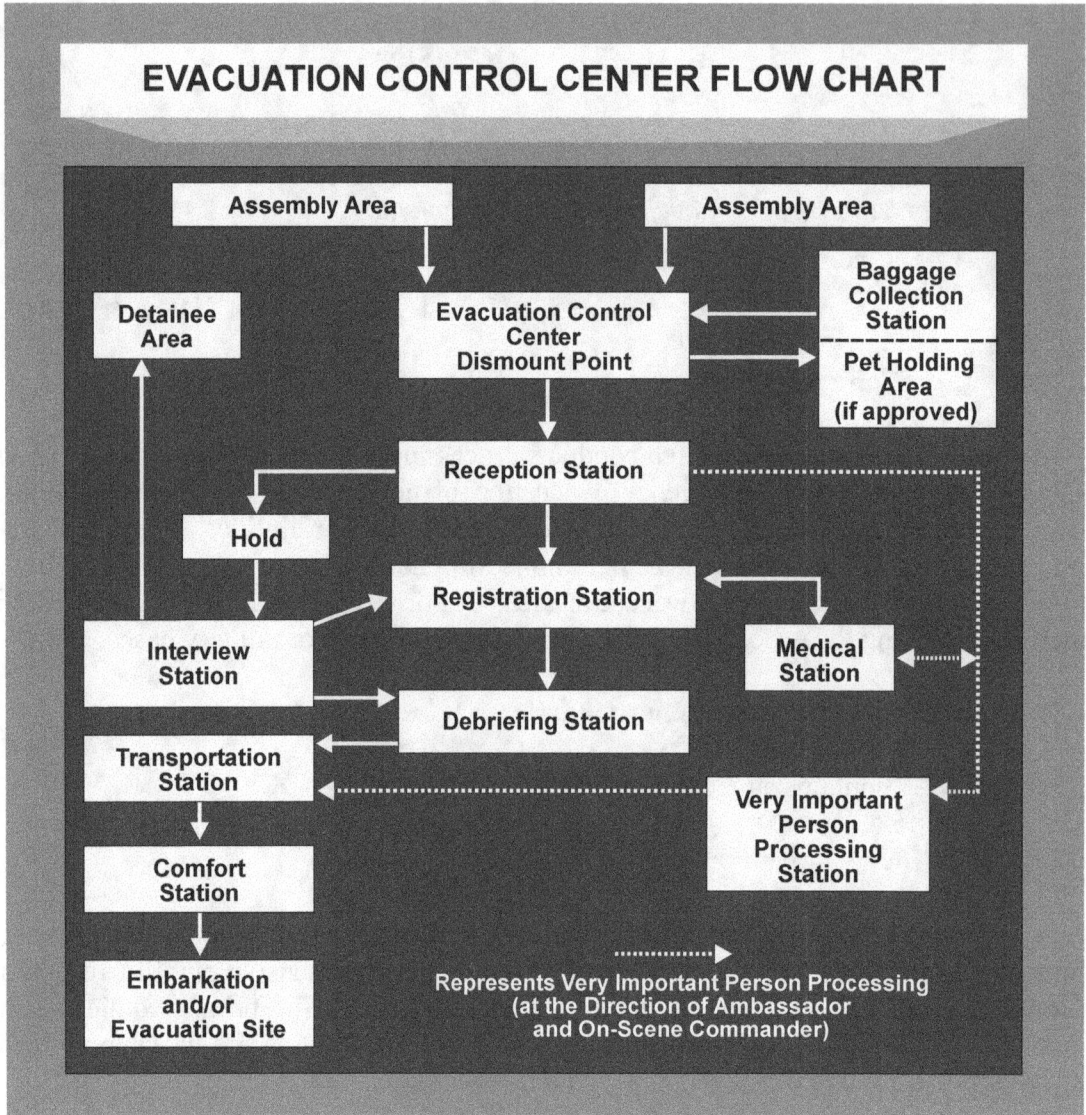

Figure VI-1. Evacuation Control Center Flow Chart

(5) Provide interpreters for bilingual information at control sites.

(6) Upon initial screen, use tags for visual identification.

(7) Establish provisions for searching women, children, and disabled and/or injured.

(8) Use DOS personnel of the same sex as evacuees to conduct searches.

(9) Have medical personnel present.

(10) Have RST personnel present.

(11) Establish procedures (separate desk or room) for USG employees or dependents, private US citizens, and TCNs. If required, a very important person (VIP) registration station should be made available.

(12) Ensure CI and human intelligence (HUMINT) elements are present to conduct intelligence collection, debriefing, screening, and threat vulnerability assessments.

(13) Organize evacuees and ensure the following:

(a) Establish a single POC between the evacuee group and the JFC.

(b) Contact civic officials to increase control and response for the evacuation.

(14) Request additional diplomatic license plates for authorized use by JTF personnel during the operation.

(15) Determine the need for EOD personnel (HN or US military).

(16) Establish a veterinary support facility, if DOS allows pet evacuation.

c. **Onboard Ship.** Should the environment on land preclude the use of an in-country ECC, evacuees may be processed onboard a ship. If it is a US Navy ship, the responsibility for processing evacuees rests with the ship's commanding officer. The activities of the ECC will be accomplished onboard ship. Accounting and manifesting should be accomplished by using the NTS.

d. **Minimum Processing Requirements.** Prior to implementation of minimum evacuee processing procedures, the procedures will be coordinated between the ambassador and the GCC. Minimum processing requirements are used in those cases when there is a documented concern for the protection and safety of evacuees and the evacuation force. The procedures used will meet the following guidelines:

(1) Force protection will not be compromised to expedite processing.

(2) Processing of persons with life threatening medical problems will be expedited.

(3) All evacuees will be screened for verification of identity and documentation as well as prioritization. Classification, priorities, and considerations for evacuees are explained in paragraph 5, "Classification, Priorities, and Considerations for Evacuees."

(4) A registration station should be established, and manifesting should be accomplished by using the NTS.

4. Evacuation Control Center Organization and Operations

a. The three guiding principles for any ECC are accuracy—all personnel are accounted for; security—evacuees and the evacuation force are safeguarded from all threats; and speed—processing must be accomplished quickly and efficiently. As the marshalling teams bring the evacuees to the ECC, the processing center assumes control of the evacuees. The purpose is to prepare the evacuees for eventual overseas movement to a temporary safe haven or the United States. All evacuees should be screened to certify identification and to ensure that documentation is accurate and all information provided is current. Representatives from the embassy's consular affairs office should be in the ECC to determine the eligibility of questionable evacuees. If evacuees arrive without escort, processing personnel should verify their identity and eligibility for evacuation prior to allowing the evacuees to enter the ECC. The processing center performs the necessary screening, registration, medical, and transportation functions to ensure an orderly evacuation and consists of the following:

b. **Headquarters Section.** The HQ section is responsible as follows:

(1) Plans, organizes, and supervises the operation of the ECC.

(2) Maintains liaison with local representatives of DOS and other agencies involved in the evacuation.

(3) Advises the JFC on the progress of the evacuation.

(4) Maintains communications with all elements of the evacuation force to include ships, controlled aircraft, remote sites, evacuation vehicles, DOS personnel, HN security forces, and the ECC.

c. **Reception Station.** The reception station personnel collect all available information from the marshalling teams who escort the evacuees. Information from the marshalling team's log book is valuable because it may reduce the processing time. The evacuees should be moved into a holding area where the following should be accomplished:

(1) Receive, search, segregate, and brief incoming evacuees in conjunction with DOS representatives. The initial briefing should provide sufficient information to ease fears about the evacuation process. It should include the following:

(a) Summary of the reasons for the evacuation.

(b) Stations through which the evacuees will process.

(c) Need for an inspection of personnel and baggage.

(d) What support to expect at the temporary safe haven.

(e) What to expect upon arrival in the United States.

(f) What the repatriation center will provide.

(g) Amnesty opportunity for any restricted items.

(h) Explanation of the procedure and requirement to establish 100 percent accountability.

(i) Pets policy.

(2) Organize evacuees into groups (maintain family integrity where possible) based on political, cultural, social, religious, etc., differences, where applicable, and proceed through a process to establish accountability of each evacuee. Use the NTS to create an evacuee roster with the following data: nationality, date of birth, evacuation classification, destination, and name, address, and/or phone number of a POC in the United States for notification.

(3) Provide an escort for groups of personnel going through the processing center. The escort should be furnished a list of names for those in their group for control purposes. VIPs and emergency medical cases should be provided individual guides if available.

(4) Inspect for restricted items. Each evacuee and all baggage should be inspected at the conclusion of the briefing. Areas used for individual inspections should be screened. Hand-held metal detectors and/or explosive detectors can expedite the inspections. All restricted items should be confiscated.

(5) Many foreign countries sell drugs over the counter that US law requires a

Successful evacuee processing begins with the initial briefing from senior Department of State representatives, which provides sufficient information to ease fears about the evacuation process.

prescription to obtain. Medical personnel on the inspection team can aid in identifying these drugs.

(6) All weapons, excluding those of authorized USG personnel, will be impounded and receipts issued to the owners. Embassy or customs officials should be consulted about the disposition of these weapons. Unless the weapons are illegal in the United States, they will be returned to the owners at the repatriation center.

(7) The persons, property, papers, and families of foreign ambassadors authorized to go to the US are exempt from search under any circumstances without specific direction from DOS. Individual registration is required for accounting and manifesting purposes.

(8) The persons, property, papers, and families of foreign diplomats (other than ambassadors) authorized passage to the United States are exempt from search. However, personal baggage may be searched if there is reasonable cause to believe that the baggage contains restricted items. All searches should be conducted in the presence of the diplomats or their authorized agent. Individual registration is required for accounting and manifesting purposes.

(9) Diplomatic pouches will not be searched.

(10) Based on reasonable belief, the JFC may refuse to evacuate any baggage suspected of containing weapons or explosives.

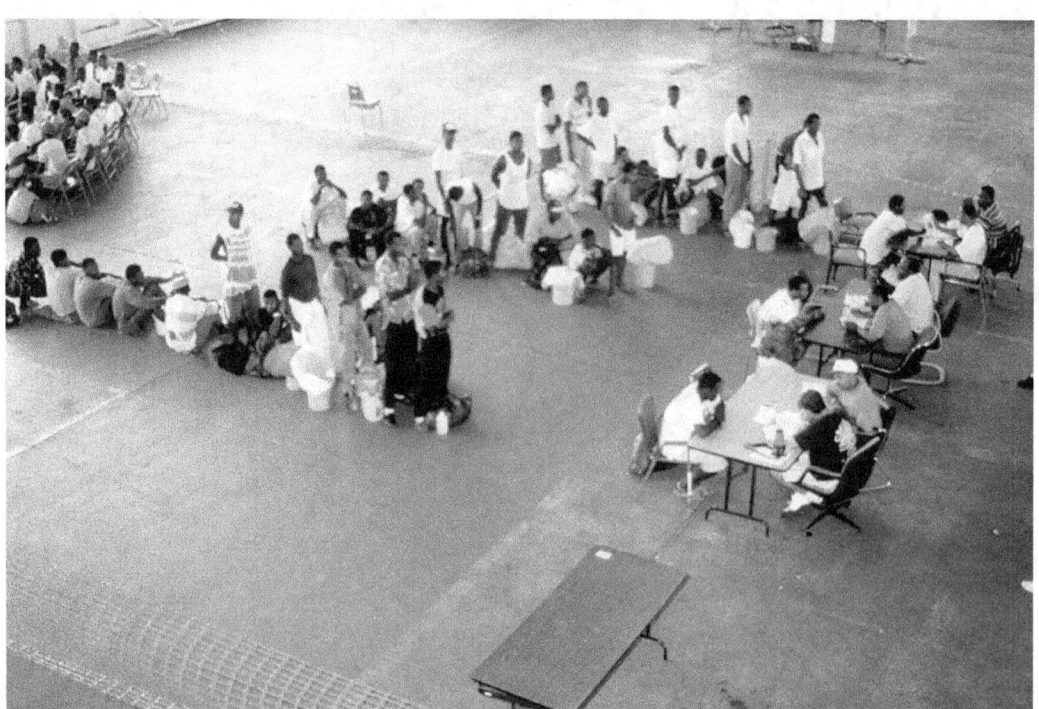

The Evacuation Control Center supports the Department of State in processing evacuees accurately, securely, and in a quick and efficient manner.

(11) Evacuees suspected of being enemy agents or criminals should be segregated and escorted to the screening station. The screening should be voluntary, but considered a prerequisite to evacuation. At the conclusion of the interviewing, the evacuees will be allowed to continue the processing, set free, or placed in a detainee area.

d. **Registration Station.** Evacuees should complete all administrative paperwork required to evacuate. When the situation allows, risks are few, and time is available, the evacuee should complete all required forms prior to leaving the ECC. However, when the security situation requires rapid movement, only the minimum essential processing for accountability and manifesting will be accomplished. **There should be no requirement for evacuees to complete all administrative paperwork as a precondition for evacuation.** Establishing initial accountability is not considered administrative paperwork. Foreign nationals must either be on the list of potential evacuees provided by the embassy or secure approval from the US embassy before they can continue processing. The ambassador or designated DOS representative will be the final authority on acceptability of evacuee identification. If there are doubts about a person's identity, the matter will be turned over to DOS and the person should not be evacuated until cleared by DOS. Registration station personnel should ensure that foreign nationals are supervised until they are cleared for evacuation or escorted outside the ECC. Military police should be available to react to any hostile incidents. Each evacuee should do the following:

(1) Prove identity by presenting a passport, dependent identification card, seaman's paper, or anything that unquestionably establishes US citizenship.

(2) Provide information to the registration clerks concerning background and personal history. DOS's EPH provides for a standard one-page OF (Optional Form)-28, Evacuee Documentation Card, that has three carbon copies. All critical information is recorded on the form, to include personal data, health and citizenship status, privacy warning, and promissory note. The original of the form remains at the ECC while the copies can be used as boarding passes for evacuation transportation and for in-processing at the temporary safe haven.

(3) Receive a copy of DD Form 2585, Repatriation Processing Center Processing Sheet (see Appendix F, "Repatriation Processing Center Processing Sheet"), which should be completed before arrival at the repatriation center. A complete listing and explanation of all suggested NEO packet items, to include all of the documentation required for each evacuee and/or family to receive proper safe haven entitlements and process through the repatriation center expeditiously, may be found in the *Joint Plan for DOD Noncombatant Repatriation.*

e. **NEO Tracking System.** The NTS is an automated data processing hardware and software package designed to assist JFCs in maintaining visibility and accountability of noncombatant evacuees as they proceed through the evacuation pipeline. The NTS uses the paradigm of assigning a bar code to a package and then tracking the package through to its delivery. The NTS provides near real-time accountability of evacuees by enabling operators to create and maintain a database of information (bar code) for each evacuee (to include pets) as they enter, proceed through, and finally exit the NEO process at a repatriation site or other exit point. Operators input data by hand into the NTS from sources such as the DD Form 2585, Repatriation Processing Center Processing Sheet, or data is electronically transferred from military identification cards and passports that meet current electronic transfer standards. The NTS collects data from "smart cards" and other electronic data sources and is capable of exchanging data with other DOD systems such as the global transportation network and the Automated Repatriation and Recording System. Web-based access is possible. Access to the NTS should be available at the ECC processing center when DOD assists DOS in an evacuation.

f. **Debriefing Station.** This station is optional, depending on the situation and the time available to conduct the evacuation. It should be staffed by personnel who are trained to debrief/screen and are able to speak the local language. Suitable personnel include, but are not limited to, CI, HUMINT, security, and linguists. Each evacuee should be debriefed to obtain information that may affect the evacuation force, its mission, the evacuees, or other USG activities in the country. Areas of interest might include the following:

(1) Locations of other potential evacuees.

(2) Changes in the political situation.

(3) Movements and activities of indigenous groups, entities, and parties that might oppose the evacuation.

(4) The true intent of a threatening third party—consider the following:

(a) Capability and likelihood of carrying out a threat.

(b) Can the third party be influenced?

(c) Can the potential threat be stopped or countered?

(5) Information/sources of activity, criminal behavior, or civil disorder that affect the NEO:

(a) Evacuation routes that are being blocked off or have been closed.

(b) Physical abuse or assault being done to deter evacuation.

(c) Counterfeiting activities that are targeting required evacuation documentation.

(d) Type of weapons being used by personnel interfering with evacuation.

(e) Use of vehicles or armored vehicles to interfere with evacuation.

(f) Public messages or fliers that gave wrong information for evacuation procedures.

(g) Criminal groups or organizations that are interfering with evacuation.

(6) Information/sources from people with unknown boxes or packages being transported for pay, favors, or gifts.

g. **Medical Station.** The medical station provides emergency medical treatment and immunizations required by the safe haven country. As required, injured or ill evacuees may proceed through the medical station for first aid and to identify medical conditions that may have an effect on the evacuation process. Serious medical cases receive top priority for evacuation. However, the medical officer ensures that any seriously ill, injured, or wounded persons complete processing prior to being evacuated. Medical personnel should:

(1) Screen to determine if an evacuee requires emergency medical treatment or evacuation.

(2) Perform emergency treatment as required.

(3) Isolate persons infected with contagious diseases.

(4) Perform disease and annoyance vector control.

h. **Chemical, Biological, Radiological, and Nuclear (CBRN) Medical Management.** The medical management of casualties resulting from infectious disease exposure to CBRN hazards, in particular biological agents, will require significant augmentation and specialized considerations to care for the resultant casualties. AE capabilities for CBRN-contaminated and contagious casualties are very limited. The JFC should consult with USTRANSCOM to determine whether casualty evacuation or treatment in place is appropriate.

For additional information on the unique aspects of CBRN medical management, including decontamination and triage, collective protection, and patient evacuation, refer to JP 3-11, Operations in Chemical, Biological, Radiological, and Nuclear (CBRN) Environments.

i. **Transportation Station.** Transportation personnel prepare each group of evacuees for embarkation aboard aircraft, ships, or surface vehicles. Some considerations are as follows:

(1) Coordinate surface and/or air transportation to include movement of personnel to the evacuation area, transportation of evacuees to designated aircraft and/or landing craft, and internal evacuation site requirements.

(2) Provide loading control personnel to supervise loading of personnel aboard vehicles, aircraft, and/or landing craft.

(3) Establish the manifest of all embarked personnel showing destination and identifying information by scanning evacuee's wrist bracelet using NTS.

(4) Organize evacuees into transportation groups (chalks), issue boarding passes for aircraft, and verify baggage tags.

(5) If NTS is not used, ensure that information on the passenger manifest agrees with information provided on the evacuee register.

(6) Ensure sufficient transportation assets to transport evacuees and their baggage to the point of embarkation.

(7) Establish a pet holding area, if required.

j. **Comfort Station.** The comfort station is a controlled access area for evacuees while they await evacuation transportation. Comfort station personnel should make the evacuees' stay as untroubled as possible and provide some degree of privacy. Some considerations are as follows:

(1) Evacuees should be segregated by transportation groups (chalks). A manned cordoned off area may be required.

(2) Sufficient shelter, cots, blankets, food, water, and infant supplies.

(3) Sufficient sanitation facilities.

(4) Senior personnel, medical personnel, and RSTs available to counsel evacuees, especially families with young children.

(5) Medical personnel should observe evacuees for any visible symptoms of illness/injury that may impede or disrupt the NEO.

(6) Male and female personal items.

5. Classification, Priorities, and Considerations for Evacuees

a. **General.** For organizational purposes all evacuees receive a number priority and classification designator. These categorizations are critical to the smooth execution and success of the operation and are used when identifying, moving, and locating evacuees. The JTF staff should keep abreast of changes in the projected number of potential evacuees by receiving periodic updates from the embassy's staff. These updates will be provided in the form of a total number for all evacuees and number by category.

b. **Classification.** The following system, shown in Figure VI-2, governs priorities of evacuations. A priority designator includes a combination of a Roman numeral and capital letter indicating major and minor priorities assigned to each individual. Designated other persons for whom the US provides evacuation assistance are classified using applicable criteria within major and minor categories.

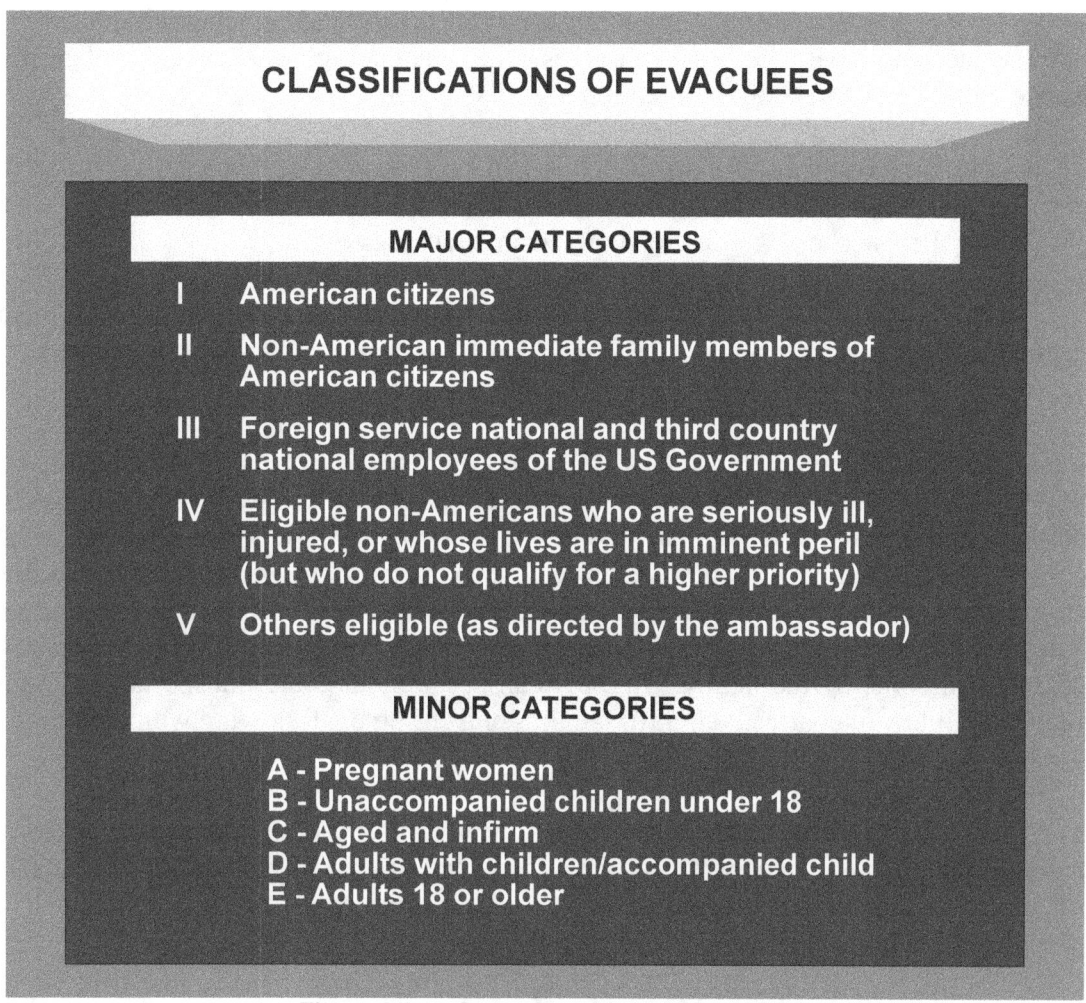

Figure VI-2. Classifications of Evacuees

c. **First Priority.** US citizens in the following order (within each category, other priorities may exist for those with certain medical conditions that require transport to save life, limb, or eyesight):

(1) Those with current identification such as passports, birth certificates, DOD identification cards, seaman's papers, air crew cards, and anyone designated as first priority by the ambassador, regardless of national affiliation. The ambassador is the final authority.

(2) Those with expired US passports less than 10 years old.

(3) Those with expired US passports over 10 years old.

d. **Guidelines.** Some guidelines for interaction with evacuees are as follows:

(1) Evacuees are not detainees.

(2) The minimum force required should be used.

(3) Evacuation can be an unsettling experience, especially for children and families who have become separated. As a rule, presenting a patient, courteous, and professional attitude will do much to calm the situation and all evacuees.

(4) Depending on the situation, personal baggage may be limited.

(5) People should not be separated from their baggage.

(6) Baggage will be searched for firearms, explosives, ammunition, or items declared to be restricted items. Be considerate but firm; the safety of personnel is paramount.

(7) The ambassador should establish a policy concerning pets. Whenever possible, allow pets to accompany evacuees except in situations where lives will be jeopardized or security compromised. If pets arrive for evacuation, a pet holding area should be established. Although DOD authorities have gone to great effort to make plans to evacuate pets, this may not be feasible in all evacuations, and families must make plans for their pets to stay behind or be transported commercially. The costs of any commercial transport of pets must be borne by the family. If DOD can accommodate the transportation of pets through a military or chartered aircraft, families must bring the following with their pets to the assembly area.

(a) Separate airline-approved pet containers for each animal except those with nursing litters. Note: Crates with watering bowls and limited towels and/or blankets are preferred. Do not include rawhide chew toys. Dog and cat food will be available at intermediate staging areas and US repatriation sites.

(b) Movement orders and health and vaccination certificates should be attached in a waterproof bag to the outside of the crate. Written medication or special care instructions should be provided to personnel at the assembly point.

(c) Dogs and cats should wear collars with owner identification, and pet owners shall have a leash or harness for their pet and muzzles for agitated or aggressive animals.

(d) Pets other than dogs or cats also must be in airline-approved crates. Families should secure all permits required to import the pet to the safe haven. A copy of the permit plus any health or vaccination certificates should be attached to the crate in a waterproof bag. Additionally, special food requirements sufficient to cover the duration of the evacuation process must accompany the pet.

(e) Owners of any exotic pets must provide warnings and handling instructions and include same on any container.

(8) Personnel must not accept gifts, tips, bribes, or any personal favor. All personnel must be aware of this prohibition.

(9) All questions about an evacuee should be referred to DOS representative.

(10) Persons of higher priority may elect evacuation in a lower priority to avoid separating families. **If it is necessary to MEDEVAC a member of a family, the entire family will be evacuated medically** (dependent on time constraints and space availability).

(11) Well-established liaison with local airport security and ambulance service is essential.

(12) Medical personnel and RST personnel should consider wearing distinctive clothing or markings to aid in identification.

(13) When possible, patients should be given written instructions for medical care, especially care for children.

e. **Request for Political Asylum or Temporary Refuge.** International law and customs have long recognized the humanitarian practice of providing temporary refuge to anyone, regardless of nationality, who may be in imminent physical danger. It is the policy of the US to grant temporary refuge in a foreign country to nationals of that country or to TCNs solely for humanitarian reasons when extreme or exceptional circumstances put in imminent danger the life or safety of a person, such as pursuit by a mob. The officer in command of an aircraft, ship, station, or activity decides which measures can prudently be taken to provide temporary refuge. No information shall be released to the media concerning requests for political asylum until cleared by DOS. Any requests by foreign governments for the return of an individual must be reported to the DOS representative. Until determination is made by DOS, safeguard those who have requested political asylum or temporary refuge. Do not release personnel against their will to a third party force. The safety of JTF personnel and security of the unit must be taken into consideration along with the following:

(1) Grant temporary refuge in cases where the requesting individual is in imminent danger, irrespective of whether political asylum or temporary refuge is requested.

(2) Let DOS representatives handle political asylum requests through the appropriate channels.

(3) Establish procedures to notify the GCC of actions taken in cases of requests for political asylum.

See Appendix B, "Legal Considerations," for additional guidance on political asylum or temporary refuge.

Intentionally Blank

CHAPTER VII
INTERMEDIATE STAGING BASE AND SAFE HAVEN OPERATIONS

"The work of organization is never done, and the structure has to be continually adapted to new and anticipated conditions."

Ralph J. Cordiner, Chief Executive Officer
General Electric Company, 1950–1964

1. Intermediate Staging Base

a. An ISB is a temporary location used to stage forces prior to inserting the forces into the HN. Use of an ISB during deployment provides the JFC many advantages over deploying directly from the home station. The ISB becomes more important as the distance from the home station increases and the likelihood of hostilities increase. The ISB may be located in another country close to where the evacuation is taking place or may be any ship under US control. Ideally, the ISB will also function as a temporary safe haven, if one is required. The ISB may also serve as an airfield for support forces, such as additional airlift for unforeseen movement requirements and/or combat forces (such as air units capable of offensive attacks and airborne infantry units) in the event that a forcible entry is required.

b. **Advantages.** The items shown in Figure VII-1 can be accomplished at the ISB.

ADVANTAGES OF AN INTERMEDIATE STAGING BASE

⊠ The joint force commander can finalize evacuation plans

⊠ The joint task force (JTF) staff can gather additional information, including intelligence, information on criminal activity, and information for counterintelligence

⊠ The JTF can conduct rehearsals and briefings

⊠ Units have the opportunity to redistribute and finalize loads

⊠ Personnel can recuperate after a long trip from their deploying base

⊠ A reaction force or additional security personnel can pre-stage for contingency operations

⊠ It can function as the temporary safe haven for the operation

Figure VII-1. Advantages of an Intermediate Staging Base

c. **Coordination.** When an ISB is located in a country other than the United States, DOS is responsible for coordinating with the government of that country. If the ISB is an established US base in a foreign country, using the ISB as a staging point for launching forces into another country can pose significant political problems. Since ISBs are typically airfields or seaports, the supported GCC should query USTRANSCOM for available transportation infrastructure on-hand information related to facilities and sites being considered as likely ISBs.

d. **Selection Criteria.** Selecting an ISB for the NEO is a time-sensitive issue. DOS will inform the GCC of the location and availability of countries for establishment of possible ISBs. The JFC should ensure the ISB meets operational requirements and advise DOS of these requirements. The ISB should meet the following criteria:

(1) Be capable of handling the aircraft or ships used in the evacuation.

(2) Possess effective communication with JTF and combatant command HQ, advance party, ECC, temporary safe haven, ISB, and the embassy.

(3) Have adequate facilities for billeting, messing, provision of emergency medical treatment, and sanitation for the evacuation force and evacuees if used as the temporary safe haven.

(4) Possess repair and refuel capability for aircraft.

(5) Have storage facilities for perishables; petroleum, oils, and lubricants; medical supplies; and ammunition.

(6) Be close to major medical facilities, if possible.

(7) Be located to provide maximum possible OPSEC.

(8) Have overflight and access rights IAW DOD 4500.54-G, *Department of Defense Foreign Clearance Guide*.

(9) Have a PA contingency plan for planned or "no-notice" media presence.

(10) Be close enough to the evacuation site that aircraft or ships used in the evacuation can transit without refueling.

(11) Have adequate local and area security forces to protect US personnel and equipment. This protection could be accomplished either by the HN or by security forces from the deployed ISB support element.

e. **Composition.** The composition of the ISB force depends on what support is required and what is already on site at the ISB. An ISB at an established, modern facility requires substantially less than one at a lesser developed location. Some considerations for the ISB force are as follows:

(1) Maintenance and service personnel for aircraft.

(2) Liaison with the embassy and civilian agencies (police, military, customs, and others as required).

(3) Interpreters.

(4) Facilities for maintenance, refueling, billeting, messing, and sanitation.

(5) Contracts for local services and supplies.

(6) Local security.

(7) Air traffic control and airfield management.

(8) Movement control.

(9) HN medical infrastructure.

(10) Overflight rights.

2. Temporary Safe Haven Site

a. A temporary safe haven, designated by DOS, is a location in an area or country to which evacuees may be moved quickly and easily. Ideally, the safe haven will be in the United States; however, circumstances may exist that require an intermediate or temporary safe haven. Adequate transportation may not be available to move all evacuees directly from the evacuation sites to the United States. An intermediate safe haven may be a US Navy ship; however, the evacuees should be removed from the ship to land-based safe havens (in the United States or a third country) as quickly as possible. If a temporary safe haven is required, DOS coordinates with the government in the country where it will be located. Coordination for the use of facilities, customs requirements, security, transportation, and billeting is required. While arranging for support of evacuees is the responsibility of DOS, commanders in theater must be prepared to assist DOS in arranging for life support of evacuees at the temporary safe haven. In crisis situations, DOD has greater capacity, and often experience, in arranging for contracted support.

b. The following factors should be considered when selecting a site:

(1) OPSEC before and during the evacuation operation to ensure mission success and prevent undue pressure against the temporary safe haven government.

(2) Capability to communicate with the ECC, JTF HQ, and the embassy.

(3) Airfield or port capacity suitable for the aircraft or ships being used, both for the evacuation and later onward movement for the evacuees. Consideration should be given to the following:

(a) Twenty-four-hour operations for the airfield and port.

(b) Availability of HN controllers to control the airfield and the requirement for JTF controllers.

(c) Balance of airflow restrictions against anticipated dates and timing of anticipated air flow.

(d) Total numbers and types of aircraft involved in the operation.

(e) Condition of aircraft parking areas.

(f) Length, width, and condition of runways and taxiway.

(g) Airfield search and rescue, security, fire fighting, and logistic support.

(h) Airfield maintenance support.

(i) Capabilities of airfield facilities.

(j) Channel and harbor depth.

(k) Berthing space, pier information, and location of anchorages.

(l) Types and capabilities of tugs.

(m) Availability of equipment to load and/or offload ships, if required.

(n) Climatological, meteorological, and oceanographic considerations.

(4) Proximity to major transportation hubs.

(5) Adequate billeting, rations, and potable water for evacuees and the temporary safe haven force.

c. Although the temporary safe haven operates under the authority of the host government, it may not have the goodwill of the local population. It may be a prime target for terrorism and riots. The JFC should plan for such situations and protect the evacuees and the JTF personnel.

3. Alternate Safe Haven

a. During a NEO, evacuees may prefer to reside somewhere other than the designated safe haven (normally CONUS). Most often the request is for the family to reside overseas in the spouse's native country. At the time of the evacuation, the Office of the Secretary of Defense will designate the individual with the authority to approve requests for alternate safe havens.

b. Families who seek alternate safe havens should be cautioned that, as temporary residents in foreign safe haven locations, they do not have official status with the HN. They may enter the HN as tourists, and may need visas or be required to pay taxes on their personal property. Sponsors should be advised that the SOFA is for the sponsor and accompanying family members, not for isolated family members. Additionally, family members who choose a safe haven in a foreign country are no longer command sponsored and may not be authorized to use exchange or medical facilities, DOD schools, base housing, or US mail services. The sponsor's request for an alternate family safe haven therefore must be justified and must show why the designated safe haven is not suitable for the evacuees.

4. Organization and Functional Considerations

a. The temporary safe haven force, organized similarly to the ECC's processing section, operates under the control of the JFC in coordination with the appropriate DOS representative. It should deploy no later than the evacuation force; however, logistic requirements to support a large number of evacuees may require that it deploy earlier. A limited security force can provide necessary internal and perimeter security. The force may consist of the following elements.

b. **Command Group.** The command group coordinates the overall operation and should consist of the commander, executive officer, staff noncommissioned officer in charge, communications officer, family center staff, chaplain, LNOs, and interpreters. The family center staff provides and coordinates human and social service support for evacuees. The RST personnel plan and coordinate comprehensive religious support for the safe haven force and evacuees. The LNOs and interpreters maintain contact with the US embassy and the host government. The command group:

(1) Plans, organizes, and supervises the operation of the temporary safe haven.

(2) Maintains liaison with local DOS representatives and other agencies that may be involved with the operation.

(3) Advises the JFC on the progress of the temporary safe haven operations.

(4) Establishes procedures for government officials and TCNs if not previously established by the CJTF.

(5) Establishes provisions for searching women and children as well as disabled and injured persons.

c. **Reception Team.** This team consists of a briefing section and a PA section.

(1) **Briefing Section.** This section should brief the evacuees on their arrival concerning the following:

(a) Current political situation in the HN.

(b) Description and operation of the temporary safe haven.

(c) Further traveling options and arrangements.

(d) Customs requirements in the temporary safe haven.

(e) Projected departure times for flights to the United States.

(f) Restrictions applicable to evacuees while at the temporary safe haven.

(g) Medical threat surveillance related to HN.

(h) Accountability requirements and procedures.

(i) Pet policy (when applicable).

(2) **Public Affairs Section.** Release of information on the NEO or temporary safe haven operations within each country is the responsibility of the ambassador. The temporary safe haven PAO has the same responsibilities as the JTF PAO, which are provided in Chapter V, "Employment and Evacuation Operation Procedures." Temporary safe haven PAO responsibilities are as follows:

(a) Advise the temporary safe haven commander on all aspects of PA.

(b) Coordinate and supervise all PA and PA-related command information functions, to include planning and production of bulletins, newsletters, and other information media.

(c) Keep the JTF PAO advised on all aspects of PA.

(d) Distribute information pertaining to the temporary safe haven and its operations to the news media per JTF policies.

(e) Escort civilian and military news media representatives.

(f) Ensure that appropriate guidelines are in place for news media to protect the privacy of evacuees in billeting areas.

(g) Ensure that interviews of JTF personnel and evacuees are held only with the permission of the JFC and the individual concerned.

(h) Determine and disseminate JTF guidance on the release of information to the public.

d. **Processing Team.** This team does not duplicate processing completed at the ECC, but should verify that all information obtained from the evacuees is complete and correct.

(1) **Administrative Section.** This section registers and accounts for all evacuees and ensures that all information required by DOS or the JTF has been collected. The administrative section should have legal personnel advise evacuees on claims procedures and assist in relations between evacuees, safe haven personnel, and HN nationals. The following should be accomplished:

(a) Receive and register incoming evacuees, using NTS, in conjunction with DOS representatives.

(b) Maintain a roster of each evacuee who passes through the temporary safe haven. It should list the nationality, date of birth, evacuation classification, destination, and name, address, and/or phone number of a POC in the United States for notification.

(c) Provide escorts for groups of personnel. VIPs and emergency medical cases should be provided individual guides if available.

(d) Provide for safekeeping and security of valuables while evacuees wait for onward transportation to the United States.

(e) Provide assistance as needed in locating separated family members.

(2) **Transportation Section.** The transportation section is responsible for assisting in the onward movement of evacuees to their final destination. The USG does not provide funding for the movement of persons other than USG (military and civilian) employees and family members to their final destination. See Chapter IV, "Contingency and Predeployment Planning Considerations," subparagraph 6c, "Personnel Eligible for Evacuation Assistance," for additional information. Nongovernment employees evacuated by US-funded charter, whether commercial or military, are asked to sign promissory notes to cover the cost of transportation. The following transportation functions should be considered to ensure an orderly movement:

(a) Coordinate surface or air transportation for the movement of evacuees to the United States and then coordinate this movement flow with the JRCC.

(b) Coordinate movement flow of evacuees with the JRCC at the repatriation site.

(c) Provide loading control personnel to supervise loading of personnel aboard aircraft, ships, or vehicles.

(d) Maintain a manifest of all embarked personnel showing destination and identifying information.

(e) Expedite the departure of all evacuees who are sick, injured, or wounded in coordination with the medical section.

(3) **Intelligence Section.** This section may debrief each evacuee if a debriefing was not conducted at the JTF ECC. If the temporary safe haven is also acting as a temporary ISB, intelligence personnel should arrange to pass information gained from evacuees to the combatant command JIOC to advise forces who are returning to a threat area for follow-on operations.

(4) **Medical Section.** The medical section provides support to the temporary safe haven force. Additionally, this section may need to conduct evacuee medical screening if it was not performed at the ECC. Medical services may include any or all of the following functions:

(a) Determine if an evacuee requires emergency medical treatment.

(b) Perform emergency treatment as required or coordinate with a local safe haven country hospital to perform the treatment.

(c) Advise the temporary safe haven OIC on hygiene and preventive medicine.

(d) Inspect food and water obtained from local sources.

(e) Evaluate the general health of the evacuees, particularly in regard to pregnancies and the possibility of communicable diseases.

(f) Provide veterinary support for pet health care as required.

e. **Comfort Team.** This team provides logistic support for the operation. It is responsible for supplies, billeting, sanitation facilities, food, and local transportation. A contracting or purchasing officer should be assigned to coordinate services with the HN. Some considerations are as follows:

(1) Billeting is ideally accomplished through facilities or hotels provided by or contracted from the temporary safe haven country. However, the JTF may be required to establish a tent city. In this event, the temporary safe haven force arrives early enough to

accomplish this before evacuees begin arriving. The JFC may consider contracting locally for the labor and sanitation facilities.

(2) Because evacuees will normally leave the HN with little or no food supplies of their own; meals, ready to eat, can be used as a temporary solution. However, the temporary safe haven OIC should be prepared to establish a food service section to provide special diets to personnel involved in the evacuation.

(3) If the climate of the country is substantially different from the evacuee's former residence, the team may need to provide adequate clothing.

(4) Due to the situation, evacuees may have not had the opportunity to pack personal, comfort, or hygiene items prior to arriving at the evacuation site. The following is a partial list of items the evacuees may need:

(a) Baby formula.

(b) Trash bags.

(c) Baby food and/or juice.

(d) Diapers.

(e) Toilet tissue.

(f) Feminine hygiene supplies.

(g) Toothpaste and/or toothbrush.

(h) Soap.

(i) Shampoo.

(j) Razors.

(k) Laundry detergent.

(l) Sheets.

(m) Towels.

(n) Blankets.

(o) Wash bucket.

(p) Pet food (dog and cat).

f. **Scheduling Team.** This team coordinates and plans the departure of evacuees from the temporary safe haven. The scheduling team should do the following:

(1) Coordinate with the transportation section for arrangements made for leaving the temporary safe haven.

(2) Coordinate with the comfort team to transport evacuees to the points of embarkation.

(3) Manifest authorized passengers aboard military or commercial charter flights using NTS.

g. **Security Team.** This team provides, or arranges for, adequate security at the temporary safe haven site.

h. **Religious Support Team.** This team performs or provides for comprehensive religious support for the temporary safe haven site.

i. **Family Support Services.** The GCC may task a Service component that has a demonstrated capability to provide family support services to provide a team to support the temporary/intermediate safe haven.

APPENDIX A
RULES OF ENGAGEMENT AND THE LAW OF WAR

1. Rules of Engagement

a. The ROE for NEOs reflect the limited military objective to be accomplished. NEO ROE limit the use of force to force that is necessary to successfully complete the mission and provide for the self-defense of US military personnel and defense of noncombatant evacuees. Chairman of the Joint Chiefs of Staff Instruction (CJCSI) 3121.01B, *Standing Rules of Engagement/Standing Rules for the Use of Force for US Forces,* is the basic source for standing rules of engagement (SROE)/standing rules for the use of force, and Enclosure G specifically governs actions to be taken by US forces conducting a NEO. The SROE reflect the limited objective of NEO and provide the baseline from which all supplemental ROE are drafted and approved.

b. Upon receipt of an ID or warning order, the JFC immediately reviews the ROE to evaluate their impact on evacuation operations. Normally, the JFC is told in the warning order that the SROE will apply and is instructed to request specific supplemental measures as the mission dictates. Potential problems should be identified, and requests for deletion or modification of ROE are forwarded via the GCC to the issuing authority. ROE must be tailored to support mission accomplishment and may impact the choice of a CONOPS.

c. Commanders have an inherent right and obligation to use all necessary means available and to take all appropriate actions in the self-defense of their unit and other US forces in the vicinity. ROE do not diminish this right and obligation, but govern the use of force for mission accomplishment.

(1) Defensive Actions

(a) Conducted only as aggressively as necessary to protect US lives (and those of designated TCN evacuees, as authorized and tasked), property, and equipment. The use of force should be sufficient to respond decisively to hostile acts or demonstrations of hostile intent. Such use of force may exceed the means and intensity of the hostile act or hostile intent, but the nature, duration, and scope of force used should not exceed what is required.

(b) May include pursuit only until the attacker is no longer a threat to US personnel (and designated TCN evacuees), property, and equipment.

(2) Subordinate commanders should ensure that personnel are thoroughly trained in the need to use only necessary force. All personnel must be instructed as to the importance of good order and discipline when conducting NEOs.

(3) Commanders at all levels should exercise caution to use only the force necessary to provide for the successful defense of evacuees and complete the mission.

d. Ideally, ROE should allow for approval of requests to employ nonlethal weapons (such as military information support and RCAs) and for joint fire support (such as naval surface fire support and close air support). The use of joint fires, the ability to act in defense of non-US persons, and the use of RCAs should be addressed in the ROE. As stated in CJCSI 3110.07C, *Guidance Concerning Chemical, Biological, Radiological, and Nuclear Defense and Employment of Riot Control Agents and Herbicides,* the use of RCAs is restricted to US bases, posts, or US controlled portions of foreign installations where the authority to approve peacetime employment of RCAs resides with the CCDR. Use of RCAs outside of these parameters requires higher approval. See SROE for specific approval authority. Additionally, authority for the use of RCA may be obtained pursuant to Enclosure I to CJCSI 3121.01B, *Standing Rules of Engagement/Standing Rules for the Use of Force for US Forces.*

e. The use of force is normally a measure of last resort. When time and circumstances permit, forces committing hostile acts or demonstrating hostile intent should be warned and given the opportunity to withdraw or cease threatening actions. Employment of MISO assets and capabilities should be considered toward this end.

2. Law of War Principles

It is DOD policy that law of war principles govern actions to be taken by JTF personnel in defense of US personnel, selected HN personnel, and property and equipment. Some of the law of war principles to be considered during the planning process are as follows:

a. **Military Necessity.** The principle of military necessity authorizes the use of force required to accomplish the mission. However, this principle is not applied in a vacuum. It must be applied in conjunction with other law of war principles. Military necessity generally prohibits the intentional targeting of protected persons (civilians, hostile personnel who have surrendered or are otherwise "out of combat," etc.) and places (objects or places that are used for purely civilian purposes, such as hospitals, schools, and cultural property that have not been converted to or for military/hostile use) because they do not constitute legitimate military objectives in furtherance of the accomplishment of the mission.

b. **Unnecessary Suffering.** This principle requires forces to actively avoid taking action that would cause unnecessary suffering and normally applies to the legality of weapons and ammunition. Generally, weapons and ammunition that have been issued by DOD have been reviewed to ensure compliance with the law of war and this principle. However, approved weapons and ammunition also may not be used in a way that will cause unnecessary suffering or injury. A weapon or munition would be deemed to cause unnecessary suffering if, in its normal use, the injury caused by it is disproportionate to the military necessity for it, that is, the military advantage to be gained from its use.

c. **Distinction.** This principle requires that combatants be distinguished from noncombatants, and that military objectives be distinguished from protected property or protected places. Parties to a conflict shall direct their operations only against combatants and military objectives. Military objectives are combatants and those objects which by their nature, location, purpose, or use make an effective contribution to military action and whose total or partial destruction, capture or neutralization, in the circumstances ruling at the time, offer a definitive military advantage.

d. **Proportionality.** The anticipated loss of life and damage to property incidental to attacks must not be excessive in relation to the concrete and direct military advantage expected to be gained. Proportionality is a way in which a military commander must assess his or her obligations as to the principle of distinction, while avoiding actions that are indiscriminate.

Intentionally Blank

APPENDIX B
LEGAL CONSIDERATIONS

This appendix provides general information and guidance for handling legal matters that may arise during a NEO. The JFC and subordinate commanders of the evacuation and ISB should have a legal advisor attached to their staffs to advise on military and international legal matters.

1. General

a. The JFC and subordinate commanders must ensure that JTF personnel abide by the standards of international law, including the applicable law of war and Uniform Code of Military Justice (UCMJ), as well as the provisions of the operation's ROE. The JFC should establish procedures and policies for immediately reporting and investigating violations of these standards. The JFC must report all possible, suspected, or alleged violations IAW applicable DOD and Service regulations, and should notify the embassy of a suspected violation within 24 hours of learning about its occurrence.

b. **Role of JTF Legal Advisor.** The JTF legal advisor will provide guidance on legal issues involving the NEO, in coordination with higher HQ, USG agencies, NGOs, IGOs, foreign governments, and the HN government. The key emphasis will be on assisting with interpretation of and compliance with applicable US laws and regulations; relevant international agreements, including any pertinent SOFAs; and multilateral and bilateral transit agreements impacting a NEO.

c. **Legal Imperatives.** When planning and conducting a NEO, commanders must be cognizant of legal imperatives derived from US domestic law, international agreements, and customary international law, and they should consider HN law. In view of this governing framework of laws and regulations, as well as the complexity of legal issues relating to NEOs, commanders must obtain legal guidance at all phases of NEO planning and execution, particularly during the early planning stage.

d. **Legal Input for Operational Planning.** Commanders should ensure that legal advisors at all levels are full participants in all aspects of NEO planning, operational guidance and decisions, and national policy directives. Additionally, OPLANs, warning orders, commander's estimates, ROE, operation orders, executive orders, and other operational documents should be systematically reviewed by the JTF legal advisor to ensure compliance with applicable law and regulations.

2. Specific Guidance and Terminology

a. **Foreign Diplomat.** A foreign diplomat of an embassy staff authorized to go to the United States for evacuation is entitled to special treatment IAW international law. Ideally, the individual as well as personal effects and papers are not to be searched, detained, or seized. Family members are also entitled to the same immunity unless they are citizens of the United States. The diplomatic pouch of a diplomatic courier from a state recognized by the United States shall also be immune from any search, inspection, detention, or seizure by US personnel. However, foreign diplomats may be subject to inspection, under certain circumstances, for weapons or other dangerous materials prior to boarding any vehicle, ship, or aircraft. Refusal to submit to inspection may result in the individual being barred from boarding. Foreign diplomats and their family members must follow accountability and manifesting procedures.

b. **Political Asylum or Temporary Refuge.** JTF commanders may not grant political asylum to any foreign national. They may grant temporary refuge under emergency conditions when there is imminent danger to the safety, health, or life of any person. Commanders must understand that if temporary refuge is granted, Secretary of a Military Department approval is necessary to release the individual. All requests for asylum should be referred to the embassy or senior DOS representative available. CJCSI 3121.01B, *Standing Rules of Engagement/Standing Rules for the Use of Force for US Forces*, includes a specific section addressing protection and disposition of foreign nationals in the custody of US forces.

c. **Status-of-Forces Agreement.** Any SOFA between the HN and the United States should be reviewed to determine how it applies, if at all, to the current situation involving the NEO. If time permits, it should be modified as necessary prior to the JTF arrival. If no agreement exists, the embassy may negotiate a temporary agreement with the HN, if time permits, covering criminal jurisdiction, procurement, customs, and other legal matters. DOS is responsible for negotiating any SOFA changes. Given the emergency nature of the NEO, however, it is likely that no special SOFA provisions will be negotiated.

d. **Detainee Treatment.** The embassy should determine the disposition of a detainee in advance of the JTF deployment. In the absence of this determination, it is US policy to treat all detainees humanely and IAW US law, including the law of war, and applicable US policy. Anyone detained by US forces in an attempt to deter or in response to hostile action will be provided with the protections of the Geneva Convention Relative to the Treatment of Prisoners of War of 1949, until some other legal status is determined by competent authority. The embassy, with the HN, will negotiate the disposition of the detainee.

e. **Claims.** The JTF legal advisor or designated claims officer shall develop a plan for the processing and adjudication of claims against the United States. The plan will be coordinated with the appropriate embassy staff member.

f. **International Legal Considerations**

(1) **Law of War.** Traditional legal issues associated with the law of war will not normally arise in the context of a NEO, as NEOs typically occur during times of escalating confrontation short of international armed conflict. However, the protections afforded civilians, the sick, and/or the wounded under the law of war are almost universally accepted humanitarian norms respected in many cases despite the absence of

international armed conflict. NEO planning and execution should adhere as closely as possible to international law principles as a matter of consistent practice.

(2) **National Sovereignty.** The GCC and subordinate commanders must ensure that the NEO planners are aware of sovereignty of other foreign nations and do not violate the sovereignty of any nation other than the HN. NEO planners and operators must be cognizant of the potential impact of operations on relations with other nations and of all relevant international agreements, including pertinent SOFAs and multilateral and bilateral transit agreements.

g. **Legal Assistance.** Implementing plans should provide for preventive law programs designed to avoid sudden and overwhelming demands for emergency legal assistance when evacuation becomes imminent or is implemented. To the extent practical and authorized, legal assistance and advice will be made available to eligible beneficiaries at safe haven points and collection processing points, in coordination with the US diplomatic mission.

h. **Military Justice.** Military justice will be administered IAW the UCMJ, JP 1, *Doctrine for the Armed Forces of the United States,* and JP 1-04, *Legal Support to Military Operations.*

i. **Reporting Violations of the Law of War.** All possible, suspected, or alleged violations of the law of war, for which there is credible information, including conduct that would constitute a violation of the law of war if it occurred during an armed conflict, shall be reported promptly, investigated thoroughly, and, where appropriate, remedied by corrective action, as follows:

(1) With respect to possible, suspected, or alleged violations of the law of war committed by or against members of, or persons accompanying or serving with, their commands, commanders should promptly investigate, collect and evaluate evidence, and report IAW applicable DOD and Military Department guidance. Additionally, forward reports immediately through command channels. Ensure alleged law of war violations are reported by appropriate law enforcement investigators.

(2) With respect to possible, suspected, or alleged violations of the law of war committed by or against allied military or civilian personnel, commanders should conduct appropriate preliminary investigation to determine involvement of JTF personnel and report as required through US operational channels. Once a determination is made that the JTF was not involved, further US investigation will be undertaken only at the direction of the supported GCC.

(3) In all instances of reported law of war violations, make immediate message notification to the appropriate CCDR. Service component commanders should provide such notification as soon as the tactical situation permits, rather than awaiting complete investigation. Additional details may be supplied by supplemental reports.

j. Host-Nation Support

(1) The GCC and subordinate commanders must be aware of applicable basing rights and the status of US forces within the country when planning and executing a NEO. Advance coordination should be made to ensure necessary landing, embarkation, and transit rights are in place to support a given operation.

(2) Additionally, the changing political and military situation must be taken into account prior to relying on previously negotiated HNS agreements. Liaison with DOS officials responsible for the particular NEO site must be accomplished in a timely manner.

k. **Legal Review of Rules of Engagement.** In all cases in which use of force is a possibility, legal advisors shall be consulted in the planning or preexecution phases to determine the legal basis for intervention and use of force, shall review proposed ROE, and shall assess the legal risks and potential liabilities entailed under international law.

l. **Applicable Rules of Engagement.** Commanders at every level must ensure understanding of ROE by all personnel. Requests for supplemental ROE must be handled IAW the SROE.

m. **War Powers Resolution.** Operations conducted may require consultation with, or reporting to, Congress consistent with the War Powers Resolution. War Powers Resolution reports will be initiated, as required, by DOS.

APPENDIX C
NONCOMBATANT EVACUATION OPERATIONS
PLANNING CONSIDERATIONS

This appendix provides questions that may be used to provide a common framework for evacuation planning and operations. These questions may serve as focus for the detailed planning and operational dialogue between diplomats and military forces that must precede any successful evacuation operation. These questions also serve as a good starting point for GCC priority information requirement development.

1. Will the operational environment be permissive, uncertain, or hostile? If it is permissive, are unarmed hostilities expected? If it is uncertain or hostile, will pursuit forces be necessary? What is the likelihood of terrorist activities?

2. What MNFs, NGOs, or IGOs will be operating in the area?

    a. Are MNFs integrated into the JTF plan?

    b. How are plans being deconflicted if the evacuations are separate?

    c. What are the appropriate C2 arrangements if the NEO is conducted as a multinational operation?

    d. What support is available from other participating nations?

    e. What support is required by other participating nations?

3. What is the current situation in the country? In the embassy? Near the US citizens? Near the TCNs and HN personnel to be evacuated?

4. Who is the senior US official in charge of the evacuation operation?

5. Who will give the JTF permission to complete the evacuation and to leave the evacuation site?

6. What is the chain of command for US military forces?

7. What is the relationship of the GCC and subordinate commanders with the ambassador?

8. Will all US mission and/or embassy officials be leaving? If not, who will remain?

9. Who will screen the evacuees?

    a. Are there embassy personnel assigned to screen?

b. Are there any evacuees (e.g., wardens) who will be able to help with processing and screening?

c. What are the JTF requirements for screening?

d. Who will be available to physically search female evacuees?

10. Who makes the final determination of evacuee accounting prior to final evacuation departure? Will the DOD NTS be used?

11. Is the embassy's EAP available? Is it up to date?

12. Who is the primary POC within the embassy to work with the JTF on details of the operation?

13. What steps are being taken by the embassy to get the evacuees ready for evacuation?

14. Are there any members of the JTF, or anyone reasonably available, who have been in the HN recently?

15. What information is needed immediately from the evacuees?

16. Have the primary and alternate assembly areas, evacuation sites, and routes been verified and surveyed?

a. Who provides country studies for JTF with information such as LZs, concentration of US citizens, port facilities, and landing beaches? How will this information be made available to the JTF? Who is responsible for updating this information to ensure it is current?

b. What is the total number of US personnel to be evacuated?

17. Have the screening and processing areas been verified?

18. What action should be taken concerning individuals not on the list of evacuees (e.g., TCNs)? What is the total number of TCNs to be evacuated?

a. Number per priority category.

b. Identification.

19. What will be the composition of the evacuees? Will there be a cross section of those listed in the EAP?

20. If families must be separated, is there a method of identifying unaccompanied children with parents/guardians during repatriation periods (e.g., matching numbered

wrist bands if parent/guardian is with child at evacuation site, parent/guardian matching database)?

21. What discipline problems are expected from the evacuees? Who are the potential troublemakers? Do any present a possible/credible threat?

22. What action should be taken if there is an outbreak of violence among evacuees?

23. What action should be taken if someone asks for political asylum?

24. Who and how will the baggage and personal property of all evacuees be searched for weapons or explosives? It may be necessary to expedite this process in a nonpermissive or combat environment, but even in such an environment, consideration must be given to asymmetric threats.

25. What proof of US citizenship is acceptable?

26. Are there any changes in the standard priorities for evacuation?

27. Will the US embassy be able to assign evacuation priorities before it schedules evacuation?

28. What are the arrangements for evacuee housing, security, and transfer? Will protective clothing be required? Will food be required?

    a. Type.

    b. Quantity.

    c. Location.

29. Has DOS established a pet policy? Are any animals (pets) prohibited from traveling on the designated transportation? Have restrictions concerning animals been identified at the safe haven location? Is veterinary support required?

30. Will JTF search teams be sent after missing evacuees?

31. Is there any sensitive equipment or material at the embassy that will need to be evacuated or destroyed? Will personnel with requisite clearances be required to assist in evacuating or destroying sensitive equipment or material?

32. Are there procedures in place to handle claims against US civilians?

33. If required, who will provide an emergency resupply of ammunition for the advance party?

34. What cultural nuances and customs should be known by the JTF evacuation force to avoid confrontation?

35. Who are the key HN personnel and what are their attitudes toward the evacuation?

36. What unusual environmental health conditions are likely to be faced by Service members and evacuees in this location? Will medical support be available from the embassy or HN? Have MEDEVAC procedures been coordinated with the HN? Where are the HN health services?

    a. Location.

    b. Availability.

    c. Capability.

37. What is the policy concerning seriously wounded evacuees? What is the physical condition of all evacuees? Are patient evacuation assets required? If so, is there a need to pre-stage those assets nearby? What are the MEDEVAC procedures?

38. Where are the HN police forces?

    a. Location.

    b. Availability.

    c. Capability.

    d. Loyalty to the host government.

    e. Hostility to the United States.

    f. Factional infighting present.

39. Where are the HN fire services?

    a. Location.

    b. Availability.

    c. Capability.

40. Where are the HN military forces?

    a. Location.

b. Availability.

c. Capability.

d. Loyalty to the host government.

e. Hostility to the United States.

f. Factional infighting present.

41. Will the HN be providing any security for the assembly areas of evacuation sites?

a. Location.

b. Unit.

c. Size of security force.

42. What is the potential threat?

a. Size.

b. Activity.

c. Location.

d. Unit.

e. Time.

f. Equipment.

43. What are the possible enemy COAs?

a. Delay.

b. Reinforce.

c. Attack.

d. Withdraw.

44. Will interpreter support be available from the embassy or the HN?

45. What communications support will be available from the embassy and how will the communication architecture be set up to support the operations (i.e., networks, frequencies, secure equipment availability, SATCOM availability, need for relays)?

46. Can portable communications equipment be sent to the embassy to facilitate improved and secure communication?

47. Does the adversary have an EW capability that may impact friendly communications, air operations, or ground movement? Will adversaries attempt to jam or disrupt nonsecure communications?

48. Will transportation support be available from the embassy or the HN?

    a. Type. Note: If evacuees will be transported via ARG ships, consider follow-on transportation requirements to move personnel out of theater if appropriate.

    b. Location.

    c. Capacity.

    d. Condition.

    e. Operators required.

49. Who will prepare the PA plan? How often will it be updated? Who is the lead PA director? Will media representatives be evacuated?

50. Are there areas from which the media are restricted or where access is restricted? Is there a media support plan?

51. What are the ROE for the JTF?

52. What is the guidance on the use of MISO?

53. What coordination has been made with the HN media to support the NEO and/or the NEO MISO plan?

54. Will the HN media provide support for the NEO and/or the NEO MISO plan?

55. What is the role of CA in NEO?

56. Does the JTF have permission to drop sensors and insert special operation forces?

57. Have all requirements for strategic transportation system been directed to the USTRANSCOM command center and/or crisis action team?

58. What is the best means of transportation to evacuate personnel?

    a. Can commercial airlift provide more timely evacuation than deploying US military assets?

    b. Have air requirements for units and equipment been identified in the Joint Operation Planning and Execution System?

    c. Are US naval assets readily available to stage off the coast?

    d. Would commercial air carriers be willing to add charter flights for the NEO?

    e. What commercial sealift assets are available?

    f. What commercial transportation has the US embassy already contracted to assist US citizens if departing voluntarily?

    g. At what point would commercial sea or air carriers cut back or halt operations?

    h. What transportation is available on retrograde flights by USTRANSCOM controlled aircraft deploying forces to the AOR?

    i. What is the maximum on ground capacity and fuel availability at possible evacuation airports?

    j. Would the cost of meals, baggage handling, and other service requirements be incorporated into the contract?

    k. Are emergency loading waivers required to load evacuees on cargo planes or surface vessels? Note: Emergency waivers are required from USTRANSCOM to load evacuees on military aircraft not configured for passengers or not for over-water flights. Emergency waivers are also required from the Commandant, US Coast Guard, to transport evacuees on cargo vessels not configured or equipped for passengers. Under emergency conditions, both of these options may need to be considered by transportation planners.

59. Who will provide climatological, meteorological, and oceanographic information?

60. What support is available from other US sources?

61. What support is required by other US agencies?

62. Are trained EOD personnel available through the HN?

63. Are map products of the JOA and the embassy compound available? What are the sources?

64. Who controls and ensures familiarity with GIBCOs and other geographic information?

65. Which evacuees have special medical needs such as pregnancy, infectious disease, exceptional family member, or pediatric health care problems?

66. Is an ISB available? Where? How extensive are its facilities and support capabilities?

67. Will the ambassador allow an FCE to deploy?

68. What HN religious events, holy days, festivals, celebrations, or other significant religious activities will occur during the evacuation that could adversely impact the operation?

69. What HN religious sites, shrines, buildings, facilities, or other locations do JTF marshalling teams need to be aware of to avoid desecrating them and antagonizing the populace?

Possible Dilemmas

Because each NEO is unique, situations may arise that require special considerations. JTF personnel should be briefed and prepared to deal with the following:

1. Questions concerning use of deadly force or a given weapon system in a given situation. When is deadly force authorized?

2. Interpretation of the ROE.

3. Hostile detainees who present themselves or are captured by the JTF.

4. Civil disturbance, from passive resistance or civil disobedience to violence.

5. Terrorism.

6. Bomb threats and/or suicide bombers.

7. Snipers, antitank guided missiles, etc.

8. Nonambulatory evacuees, to include those with contagious diseases or possible CBRN contamination.

9. Language and/or cultural background problems.

10. Religious and/or ethnic background problems.

11. Potential evacuee's name not on list provided by the embassy but appearing to be a bona fide evacuee.

12. Deaths of evacuees and evacuation of remains.

13. Listed evacuees or unlisted potential evacuees with unknown identifications.

14. Evacuees carrying contraband and disposition of the contraband.

15. Overwhelming numbers of civilians coming to assembly areas or at the evacuation sites to request evacuation.

16. Listed evacuee refusing evacuation.

17. Evacuee attempting to give bribes to gain favor.

18. Inaccurate evacuation lists.

19. Large numbers of international journalists converging on the area.

20. Evacuees carrying large amounts of money, gold, jewelry, and other valuable items and forms of wealth.

21. Friendly EW operations' impact on local emergency communications networks.

Intentionally Blank

APPENDIX D
SAMPLE EMERGENCY ACTION PLAN CHECKLISTS

This appendix contains sample checklists based on the DOS *Emergency Planning Handbook,* 12 FAH-1. The checklists found in an embassy EAP should be the actual checklist used for NEO.

CHECKLIST FOR US MILITARY ASSISTED EVACUATION

1.   Name and title of American official in charge of the evacuation: _____
_____

2.   American officials remaining behind: (Attach list with names, means of contact).

3.   Post officials available to assist in the processing and evacuation: (Attach list—see DOS *Emergency Planning Handbook* Exhibit 120—update to show name, probable location, and means of identification and contact of officer performing each relevant function.)

4.   How many military personnel will be needed to assist in screening evacuees and where will they need to be located? _____
Who will assist the military? _____

5.   Is the operational environment permissive, uncertain, or hostile? _____

6.   Perimeter security needs: _____
Assembly areas and embarkation points: _____

7.   What security will the HN or controlling authority provide? _____
_____

8.   Are alternate evacuation, assembly, or reception sites available if required? _____
_____

Where are the GIBCOs located and who has custody of them? _____
_____

9.   Could unauthorized and/or hostile persons forcibly or surreptitiously attempt to join the evacuation? If so, what action does the post recommend? _____
_____

10. What action does the post propose if someone asks for political asylum? _____
_____

11. Will the post's OIC vouch for the baggage and personal property of all or some evacuees or should a search for weapons and explosives be conducted?_____
_____

12. Does the ambassador desire the military to physically search those evacuees that cannot be validated? _____

13. If it becomes necessary to physically search a woman, who can conduct the search?
_____

14. If the evacuation priority is different than stated in the post plan, give the modified priority: _____
_____

15. Will food be required? _____ Total meals:_____

16. Is potable water available? _____
Quantity of bottled water required:_____

17. Does the post anticipate that any Americans will refuse evacuation? _____

18. What is the policy on evacuees taking pets? _____
_____

    a. If pets are allowed to be transported, have requirements such as customs and quarantine restrictions been considered to ensure the pets will be allowed into the safe haven? _____
_____

    b. If pets are not allowed to travel, what will happen to the pets evacuees bring with them to the evacuation processing centers? _____
_____

19. Does the embassy anticipate that military personnel will be needed to search for missing evacuees? If so, in which areas are evacuees likely to be located? (Give radio call sign frequencies, if known.) _____

20. Would a search operation meet armed resistance? _____

21. Will the post need help to destroy sensitive materials or equipment? _____

22. Portable radios available to assist in assembly, movement, and control of evacuees (consider all likely points):

    How many sets? _____ Frequencies? _____ Additional needs? _____

23. Who will prepare manifests of evacuees?

Embassy: _____

Military: _____

24. Under extreme circumstances families might be separated, and there must be a method of identifying unaccompanied children with parents/guardians during repatriation periods, etc.

25. Other items that may affect NEO:

a. Travel restrictions, curfew, roadblocks.

b. Local military activities.

c. Political or security factors affecting evacuation.

d. PA considerations.

26. If interpreters are needed, can the embassy provide? _____

27. Provide updated copies of the embassy's:

a. EPH Section 1540 and exhibits for same.

b. Communications annex.

c. Logistics annex.

d. Transportation annex.

e. F-77 (Potential Evacuees) Report.

f. GIBCOs.

28. Give number of evacuees who are:

a. Wounded, injured, or ill: litter _____

b. Wounded, injured, or ill: ambulatory _____

c. Pregnant: _____

d. Any contagious diseases or infections present? _____

29. What medical assistance (to include special equipment) will be required? _____

_____

30. Breakdown of evacuees by age and sex:

      0–7 years: male _____   female _____

      8–16 years: male _____   female _____

      17–20 years: male _____   female _____

      21+ years: male _____   female _____

31. Will doctor(s) and nurse(s) be among the evacuees? _____

32. Will any influential religious or community leaders be among the evacuees? _____

_____

33. Weight and volume of any sensitive materials or equipment requiring evacuation: _____ pounds _____ cubic feet

34. Attach an intelligence estimate of the local situation and HN military status, to include possible threats to transportation assets.

ASSEMBLY AREA

LOCATION: _____ DATE: _____

Assembly Area _____ Primary _____

Embarkation Point _____ Alternate _____

1. Location: _____

2. Grid coordinates: _____

3. Reference points: _____

4. Size: _____ Estimated capacity: _____

5. Shelter: _____

6. Cooking facilities: _____ Water: _____

7. Food stocks: _____

Estimated person/days on hand: _____

8. Latrine and shower: _____

9. Security: _____

10. Control point: _____

11. Telephone: _____ Radio call sign: _____

12. Access, chokepoints: _____

    Alternates: _____

13. Nearest police station: _____

14. Nearest medical treatment facility: _____

15. Emergency power supply: _____

16. Distances to embarkation points: _____

17. If HLZ, identify: _____

_____ Sketch attached _____ Video attached _____ Photo attached

18. Availability of fuel for surface vehicles: _____

This report prepared by: _____

HELICOPTER LANDING ZONE

LOCATION: _____ DATE: _____

1. Designator: _____

2. Location: _____

3. Grid: _____

4. Reference point(s): _____

5. Dimensions: _____

6. Surface: _____

7. Obstacles: _____
_____
_____
_____

8. Recommended air approach(es): _____

9. Recommended ground approach(es): _____
_____

10. Distance(s) to assembly area(s): _____
_____
_____

11. Fuel availability: _____

12. Comments: _____
_____
_____
_____

This report prepared by: _____

_____ Sketch attached _____ Video attached _____ Photo attached

AIRFIELD SURVEY

LOCATION: _____ DATE: _____

1. Name of airfield: _____

2. Location (map coordinates): _____

3. Fuel (type and availability): _____

4. Materials handling equipment: _____

5. Elevation: _____

6. Runway length: _____

7. Runway width: _____

8. Surface composition and estimated single wheel loading factor: _____
_____
_____

9. Available parking area: _____

10. Largest aircraft accommodated: _____

11. Instrument approach facilities; navigation aids: _____

12. Aircraft obstacles: _____
_____

13. Are runways/taxiways lighted? _____

14. Communications (frequencies, call signs used): _____
_____

15. Physical security: _____

16. Is the airfield under civilian or military control? _____
_____

17. Status of commercial air traffic into and out of the airfield during the period in issue:
_____
_____

18. Does the airfield meet any USTRANSCOM accepted (e.g., International Civil Aviation Organization, NATO, Federal Aviation Administration) standards for signs, markings, and other applicable requirements? If so, which standards? _____

_____

_____

19. What is the availability of HN certified, civilian, or military air traffic controllers?

_____

20. Key contacts: _____

21. Distance from assembly area to airport:

   Primary: _____   Secondary: _____

22. Conditions of roads leading to airport: _____

_____

23. Conditions and weight limits of bridges leading to airports: _____

24. On-site assembly areas and capacity: _____

_____

25. Latrine and shower facilities: _____

26. Feeding facilities and capacity: _____

27. Text or copy of description in "Airfield and Seaplane Stations of the World": _____

_____

This report prepared by: _____

_____ Sketch attached _____ Video attached _____ Photo attached

Note: Complete a separate form for each airfield considered feasible for use during an evacuation.

SEAPORT SURVEY

LOCATION: _____ DATE: _____

1. Name of seaport: _____

2. Location (map coordinates): _____

3. Entrance restrictions and minimum anchorage: _____

4. Channel depth, depending on season: _____

5. Water depth at berths: _____

6. Tide, depending on season: _____

7. Pilots required or available: _____

8. Navigational aids: _____

9. Port or beach obstacles: _____

10. Wharf (description and capabilities): _____
    _____

11. Materials handling equipment: _____

12. Fuel (type and availability): _____

13. Physical security available and in use: _____
    _____

14. Distance from post to seaport: _____

15. Conditions of roads leading to the seaport: _____
    _____

16. Condition and weight limit of bridges leading to seaport: _____
    _____

17. On-site assembly areas and capacity: _____
    _____

18. Dining facilities and capacity: _____
    _____

19. Latrine and shower facilities: _____

20. Location of nearest medical treatment facility: _____

21. Key contacts, key personnel: _____
_____

This report prepared by: _____

_____ Sketch attached _____ Video attached _____ Photo attached

Intentionally Blank

APPENDIX E
SAMPLE NOTICE FORMS

SAMPLE STAND FAST NOTICE

NAME OF POST:_____DATE:_____

Because of the current local situation, this office recommends that Americans remain in their homes. Only the most essential outside activities should be conducted, and public areas should be avoided until the situation improves. Since there is always the possibility the situation will deteriorate and you will be required to move elsewhere, this office recommends that you promptly take the following precautions:

1.   Without hoarding, try to keep on hand a reasonable supply (7 to 10 days) of food, water, and fuel. If you have a personal automobile, be sure it is ready for immediate use; fill the gas tank and check the oil, water, tires, and battery.

2.   If your passport, exit visa, or registration with this office is not current, contact us immediately at telephone _____.

3.   Collect all important papers and documents, such as passports; birth, marriage, divorce, and naturalization certificates; inoculation cards; insurance policies; bank books; as well as US and local currency.

4.   Make or update a complete inventory of your household effects in duplicate.

5.   Prepare for each family member one suitcase (66 pounds or less) to contain, as applicable, warm clothing regardless of season, eyeglasses, babies' and children's supplies, and special medications.

6.   Listen to the local media and Voice of America, US Armed Forces Radio, or the British Broadcasting Company closely for announcements from the local government or this office.

Your warden is _____,
who can be reached at _____.

We are monitoring the situation and will provide you with further guidance. Please pass the contents of this notice to other US citizens and keep it handy for reference.

Figure E-1. Sample Stand Fast Notice

SAMPLE LEAVE COMMERCIAL NOTICE

NAME OF POST:_____DATE:_____

1.   In view of the gravity of the current local situation, this office recommends that Americans whose presence in the country is not essential, depart by commercial transportation as soon as possible.   If adult US citizens have compelling reasons for remaining in the area, we suggest that dependents depart with their pets while normal commercial facilities are still available.

2.   American citizens with valid passports and foreign dependents with valid passports or visas should not come to this office for travel arrangements. Rather, they should make their own arrangements directly with transportation companies or travel agents.

3.   Persons departing are requested to inform this office by telephone, _____, or mail of their departure plans, providing the following information: name(s), date(s) and place(s) of issuance of passports, probable date(s) and mode(s) of transportation, and names and addresses of next of kin or other point of contact in the United States or travel agents.

4.   This office cannot accept any personal or real property for protection, but will accept copies of inventories of property left in the country and attempt to arrange for protection of such property through the local authorities.

5.   American citizens without valid passports or who are unable to arrange for their own travel or that of their dependents because of insufficient funds or other reasons should report to this office as soon as possible.   They should bring with them:

   a.   American passports or other proof of US citizenship.

   b.   For non-American spouses, children, and dependents: passports or identification cards and proof of relationship (birth or marriage certificates).

6.   Please pass the contents of this notice to other US citizens and keep it handy for reference.

Figure E-2. Sample Leave Commercial Notice

SAMPLE EVACUATION NOTICE

NAME OF POST:_____DATE:_____

Because of the situation in this country, the ambassador has determined that the evacuation of all US citizens is advisable. As the operations of this office may be terminated with little or no advance warning, American citizens wishing US Government assistance should contact their wardens or this office immediately (telephone _____). The embassy/consulate is arranging chartered transportation to the United States or another safe haven. The issuance of tickets is not feasible, and all persons being evacuated will be asked to sign promissory notes to cover the cost of their transportation. The Department of State will bill evacuees later for the costs incurred. (US Government personnel and their dependents travel on official orders and therefore their respective agencies will be billed.) To provide proper protection and to help you leave safely, we ask you to follow these instructions:

1. Your warden is _____ and may be contacted at _____.

2. Your assigned assembly area is at _____.

_____ a. Please be there at _____.

_____ b. You will be told later when to report.

_____ c. Do not bring your vehicle to the assembly point.

_____ d. Bring enough food for each family member to have _____ meals.

_____ e. Cooking facilities are not available, so bring ready-to-eat food (canned items, sandwiches, etc.).

_____ f. Bring an unbreakable container with _____ quart(s) of water per person.

_____ g. Pets will be transported during this NEO and are allowed at the assembly point.

(Only checked items apply)

3. Prepare to bring with you all important personal papers (passports, inoculation cards, cash, credit cards, and checkbooks) and one suitcase (66 pounds or less) per person containing clothing suitable for the local climate as well as for a change of climate. Remember eyeglasses, special medicines, and baby/children supplies. Do not bring firearms or liquor. Pets are allowed only if specifically authorized above.

4. Adult family members should consider the possibility of becoming separated temporarily. Problems can be avoided by exchanging data concerning bank accounts, addresses, and telephone numbers of relatives in the United States, and powers of attorney.

Figure E-3. Sample Evacuation Notice

SAMPLE EMBASSY/POST CLOSING NOTICE

NAME OF POST:_____ DATE:_____

The situation in this country is such that the US Government is closing its offices here effective _____.

The embassy of _____, located at _____, will protect US interests until further notice.

We recommend that American citizens leave the country immediately. Until this office ceases operations, we will make every effort to assist US citizens still wishing to depart. Those who plan to remain should provide their names, addresses, and next of kin so this office can pass the information to the Department of State and to the _____ embassy.

Please pass the contents of this notice to other US citizens and keep it handy for reference.

Figure E-4. Sample Embassy/Post Closing Notice

SAMPLE WAIVER OF EVACUATION OPPORTUNITY

1. Agreement made, this _____ day of _____, 20_____, between _____ and the military forces of the United States.

2. Whereas the military forces of the United States agree to evacuate_____.

3. Said offer of evacuation is declined by the above named individual(s), with the understanding that the offer will not be repeated.

4. Evacuee Signature _____
   Evacuee Signature _____
   Evacuee Signature _____
   Evacuee Signature _____

Figure E-5. Sample Waiver of Evacuation Opportunity

APPENDIX F
REPATRIATION PROCESSING CENTER PROCESSING SHEET

SECTION I - TO BE COMPLETED BY THE "RESPONSIBLE PERSON"

ARE YOU ESCORTING UNACCOMPANIED MINOR CHILD(REN)? *(X one)*   [ ] YES   [ ] NO

    The designated escort is responsible for completing (to the best of their ability) a separate form for each family group they are escorting. If there is more than one child from the same family group, enter the information in Items 6 through 20 for the <u>eldest</u> child being escorted. Then, complete the family group information for each younger child in Items 23(a) through (d), as applicable.

ADDITIONALLY, ESCORTS WILL FILL OUT A SEPARATE FORM FOR THEIR OWN FAMILY GROUP.

SECTION II - TO BE COMPLETED BY THE "RESPONSIBLE PERSON"

1. AIRLINE AND FLIGHT NUMBER	2. DATE OF ARRIVAL *(YYYYMMDD)*

3. REPATRIATION CENTER

4. PROCESSING DATE *(YYYYMMDD)*	5. PROCESSING TIME *(Military)*

SECTION III - EVACUEE IDENTIFYING INFORMATION - TO BE COMPLETED BY THE "RESPONSIBLE PERSON"

6. NAME OF EVACUEE *(Last, First, Middle Initial)*

7. COUNTRY EVACUATED FROM

8. DATE OF BIRTH *(YYYYMMDD)*	9. PLACE OF BIRTH *(City, State, and Country)*

10. COUNTRY OF CITIZENSHIP

11. GENDER *(X one)*	12. SOCIAL SECURITY NUMBER
[ ] MALE [ ] FEMALE	

13. MARITAL STATUS *(X one)*

[ ] SINGLE   [ ] MARRIED   [ ] WIDOWED   [ ] SEPARATED   [ ] DIVORCED

14.a. PASSPORT NUMBER	b. COUNTRY OF ISSUE

15.a. ALIEN NUMBER	b. COUNTRY OF ISSUE

DD FORM 2585, DEC 2007   [Reset]   Page 5 of 10 Pages

Figure F-1. Department of Defense Form 2585, Repatriation Processing Center Processing Sheet

SECTION III - EVACUEE IDENTIFYING INFORMATION (Continued) (Read before completing Items 16 and 23)

(Use these tables to complete Item 16 and Item 23 (Page 7.) Choose all that apply.)

TABLE 1a - U.S. CITIZEN	TABLE 1b - FOREIGN NATIONAL	TABLE 2
CLASSIFICATION NUMBER	**CLASSIFICATION NUMBER**	**AGENCY CODE**

TABLE 1a - U.S. CITIZEN — CLASSIFICATION NUMBER

- 1a DoD: Service Member
- b DoD: Service Member Dependent and/or Family Member (Command Sponsored Dependent)
- c DoD: Service Member Dependent and/or Family Member (Non-Command Sponsored Dependent)
- 2a DoD: Civilian Employee WITH Transportation Agreement
- b DoD: Dependent of Civilian Employee WITH Transportation Agreement
- c DoD: Civilian Employee WITHOUT Transportation Agreement
- d DoD: Dependent of Civilian Employee WITHOUT Transportation Agreement
- 3a Non-DoD U.S. Government (USG): Employee
- b Non-DoD USG: Employee Dependent and/or Family Member
- 4 Citizen Residing Abroad (Child, Student, Private Business)
- 5 Tourist
- 6 Citizen on Business-Related Travel
- 7 U.S. Government Contractor

TABLE 1b - FOREIGN NATIONAL — CLASSIFICATION NUMBER

- 8 Adult Dependent of Repatriated U.S. Citizen (Foreign spouse or other adult dependent; not U.S. citizen)
- 9 Minor Dependent of Repatriated U.S. Citizen (Child born in foreign country, not U.S. citizen to date)
- 10 Non-Dependent of Repatriated U.S. Citizen (Extended family member, i.e. mother-in-law, cousin, etc.)
- 11 Non-U.S. Civilian Employee (Works for U.S. Government)
- 12 Citizen of Country Other Than U.S.
- 13 Other, None of the Above (Specify)

TABLE 2 — AGENCY CODE

- A Army
- N Navy
- F Air Force
- M Marine Corps
- G Coast Guard
- D DoD Agency
- O Other U.S. Government Agency
- X Not Applicable

16. CLASSIFICATION NUMBER(S) AND AGENCY CODE(S) *(Enter all appropriate classification numbers and agency codes from Table 1 and Table 2 that are applicable to the person named in Item 6.)*

a. CLASSIFICATION NUMBER	b. AGENCY CODE
c. CLASSIFICATION NUMBER	d. AGENCY CODE
e. CLASSIFICATION NUMBER	f. AGENCY CODE

17. NUMBER OF FAMILY MEMBERS WITH YOU

ADULTS *(Include yourself)*	CHILDREN *(Include all children)*

18. NUMBER OF ANIMALS WITH YOU *(If applicable)*

DOGS	CATS
BIRDS	OTHER

19. EMERGENCY CONTACT IN U.S.
(For person named in Item 6 above)

a. NAME *(Last, First, Middle Initial)*

b. ADDRESS *(Street, City, State/Country, ZIP Code)*

c. HOME TELEPHONE NO. *(Include Area Code)*	d. WORK TELEPHONE NO. *(Include Area Code)*	e. CELL TELEPHONE NO. *(Include Area Code)*

20. FINAL DESTINATION AND NAME OF POINT OF CONTACT (If applicable)
(If same as Item 19, enter "SAME")

a. NAME *(Last, First, Middle Initial)*

b. ADDRESS *(Street, City, State/Country, ZIP Code)*

c. HOME TELEPHONE NO. *(Include Area Code)*	d. WORK TELEPHONE NO. *(Include Area Code)*	e. CELL TELEPHONE NO. *(Include Area Code)*

21. IF U.S. DEPARTMENT OF DEFENSE MILITARY AND CIVILIAN EMPLOYEE DEPENDENTS
(For escorted unaccompanied minor children enter the sponsor's (parent/guardian) information to the best of your ability.)

a. BRANCH OF SERVICE/DOD AGENCY *(X one)*

ARMY	NAVY	AIR FORCE	MARINE CORPS	COAST GUARD	DOD AGENCY

b. NAME OF SPONSOR *(Remaining in Country) (Last, First, Middle Initial)*	c. SSN	d. RANK/GRADE

e. ORGANIZATION/ADDRESS AND MAJOR COMMAND *(Include APO#/FPO#)*

22. FINAL DESTINATION AND NAME OF ESCORT FOR UNACCOMPANIED MINOR CHILD(REN)
(Complete if applicable)

a. NAME OF ESCORT *(Last, First, Middle Initial)*

b. ADDRESS *(Final Destination of Escort) (Street, City, State/Country, ZIP Code)*

c. HOME TELEPHONE NO. *(Final Destination of Escort) (Include Area Code)*	d. WORK TELEPHONE NO. *(Final Destination of Escort) (Include Area Code)*	e. CELL TELEPHONE NO. *(Final Destination of Escort) (Include Area Code)*

DD FORM 2585, DEC 2007 Reset Page 6 of 10 Pages

Figure F-1. Department of Defense Form 2585, Repatriation Processing Center Processing Sheet (cont.)

SECTION III - EVACUEE IDENTIFYING INFORMATION *(Continued)*

23. ACCOMPANYING EVACUEES
(Fill out for each accompanying person.)

a.(1) NAME *(Last, First, Middle Initial)*	(2) SSN	(3) DATE OF BIRTH *(YYYYMMDD)*

(4) GENDER *(X one)* ☐ MALE ☐ FEMALE

(5) RELATIONSHIP TO PERSON COMPLETING FORM *(X one)* ☐ SPOUSE ☐ SON/DAUGHTER ☐ PARENT ☐ OTHER

(6) PLACE OF BIRTH *(City, State, and Country)*	**(10) CLASSIFICATION NUMBER(S) AND AGENCY CODE(S)** *(Enter all appropriate classification numbers and agency codes from Table 1 and Table 2 (shown on Page 6) that are applicable to the person named in Item a.(1).)*	
(7) COUNTRY OF CITIZENSHIP	(a) CLASSIFICATION NUMBER	(b) AGENCY CODE
(8) PASSPORT NUMBER / COUNTRY OF ISSUE	(c) CLASSIFICATION NUMBER	(d) AGENCY CODE
(9) ALIEN NUMBER / COUNTRY OF ISSUE	(e) CLASSIFICATION NUMBER	(f) AGENCY CODE

b.(1) NAME *(Last, First, Middle Initial)*	(2) SSN	(3) DATE OF BIRTH *(YYYYMMDD)*

(4) GENDER *(X one)* ☐ MALE ☐ FEMALE

(5) RELATIONSHIP TO PERSON COMPLETING FORM *(X one)* ☐ SPOUSE ☐ SON/DAUGHTER ☐ PARENT ☐ OTHER

(6) PLACE OF BIRTH *(City, State, and Country)*	**(10) CLASSIFICATION NUMBER(S) AND AGENCY CODE(S)** *(Enter all appropriate classification numbers and agency codes from Table 1 and Table 2 (shown on Page 6) that are applicable to the person named in Item b.(1).)*	
(7) COUNTRY OF CITIZENSHIP	(a) CLASSIFICATION NUMBER	(b) AGENCY CODE
(8) PASSPORT NUMBER / COUNTRY OF ISSUE	(c) CLASSIFICATION NUMBER	(d) AGENCY CODE
(9) ALIEN NUMBER / COUNTRY OF ISSUE	(e) CLASSIFICATION NUMBER	(f) AGENCY CODE

c.(1) NAME *(Last, First, Middle Initial)*	(2) SSN	(3) DATE OF BIRTH *(YYYYMMDD)*

(4) GENDER *(X one)* ☐ MALE ☐ FEMALE

(5) RELATIONSHIP TO PERSON COMPLETING FORM *(X one)* ☐ SPOUSE ☐ SON/DAUGHTER ☐ PARENT ☐ OTHER

(6) PLACE OF BIRTH *(City, State, and Country)*	**(10) CLASSIFICATION NUMBER(S) AND AGENCY CODE(S)** *(Enter all appropriate classification numbers and agency codes from Table 1 and Table 2 (shown on Page 6) that are applicable to the person named in Item c.(1).)*	
(7) COUNTRY OF CITIZENSHIP	(a) CLASSIFICATION NUMBER	(b) AGENCY CODE
(8) PASSPORT NUMBER / COUNTRY OF ISSUE	(c) CLASSIFICATION NUMBER	(d) AGENCY CODE
(9) ALIEN NUMBER / COUNTRY OF ISSUE	(e) CLASSIFICATION NUMBER	(f) AGENCY CODE

d.(1) NAME *(Last, First, Middle Initial)*	(2) SSN	(3) DATE OF BIRTH *(YYYYMMDD)*

(4) GENDER *(X one)* ☐ MALE ☐ FEMALE

(5) RELATIONSHIP TO PERSON COMPLETING FORM *(X one)* ☐ SPOUSE ☐ SON/DAUGHTER ☐ PARENT ☐ OTHER

(6) PLACE OF BIRTH *(City, State, and Country)*	**(10) CLASSIFICATION NUMBER(S) AND AGENCY CODE(S)** *(Enter all appropriate classification numbers and agency codes from Table 1 and Table 2 (shown on Page 6) that are applicable to the person named in Item d.(1).)*	
(7) COUNTRY OF CITIZENSHIP	(a) CLASSIFICATION NUMBER	(b) AGENCY CODE
(8) PASSPORT NUMBER / COUNTRY OF ISSUE	(c) CLASSIFICATION NUMBER	(d) AGENCY CODE
(9) ALIEN NUMBER / COUNTRY OF ISSUE	(e) CLASSIFICATION NUMBER	(f) AGENCY CODE

NOTE: If there are more than 4 accompanying family members, use additional copies of Page 7.

DD FORM 2585, DEC 2007

Reset | Page 7 of 10 Pages

Figure F-1. Department of Defense Form 2585, Repatriation Processing Center Processing Sheet (cont.)

SECTION III - EVACUEE IDENTIFYING INFORMATION (SERVICES) (Continued)		
24. IF NO SERVICES ARE NEEDED, X THIS BLOCK ➝		
25. SERVICES NEEDED (X all that apply)		

CLOTHING

HOUSING	PERMANENT	TEMPORARY

MEDICAL

DOD INFORMATION

DOD LEGAL SERVICES

CHILD CARE

FEDERAL CIVILIAN PERSONNEL ASSISTANCE

LOCATOR ASSISTANCE FOR OTHER FAMILY MEMBERS

TRANSPORTATION TO ONWARD DESTINATION

FINANCIAL ASSISTANCE

MENTAL HEALTH

GENERAL INFORMATION

CHAPLAIN ASSISTANCE

FUNERAL ASSISTANCE

DOD RELOCATION INFORMATION

TRANSLATOR (indicate language)

OTHER (Specify)

26. ADDITIONAL REMARKS

STOP HERE.

DD FORM 2585, DEC 2007   Reset   Page 8 of 10 Pages

Figure F-1. Department of Defense Form 2585, Repatriation Processing Center Processing Sheet (cont.)

SECTION IV (ITEMS 27 - 36) - TO BE COMPLETED BY REPATRIATION PROCESSING CENTER DEPARTMENT OF HEALTH AND HUMAN SERVICES (DHHS) STAFF					

27. IF NO SERVICES ARE REQUIRED/WERE PROVIDED, X THIS BLOCK ———————▶

28. SERVICES PROVIDED BY DHHS

(1) SERVICES	(2) COSTS		(3) TOTAL
a. CASH ASSISTANCE	PERSONS X	DOLLARS =	0.00
b. ONWARD TRANSPORTATION	PERSONS X	DOLLARS =	0.00
	PERSONS X	DOLLARS =	0.00
c. TEMPORARY LODGING AND PER DIEM	PERSONS X DAYS X	DOLLARS =	0.00
d. MISCELLANEOUS *(Specify)*		=	
		=	
		=	
		=	
	29. TOTAL COSTS	=	0.00

30. HAS EMERGENCY MEDICAL ASSISTANCE BEEN PROVIDED OFF-SITE? *(X one)* ———————▶ YES NO

31. ADDITIONAL REMARKS

SECTION V - CLOSING QUESTIONS - TO BE COMPLETED BY REPATRIATION PROCESSING CENTER DEPARTMENT OF HEALTH AND HUMAN SERVICES (DHHS) STAFF	*(X one)*	
	YES	NO
32. HAS REPATRIATE BEEN GIVEN A HEALTH AND HUMAN SERVICES WELCOME BROCHURE?		
33. DOES THIS PERSON/FAMILY NEED A LOAN FOR TEMPORARY ASSISTANCE BECAUSE HE/SHE/THEY ARE WITHOUT RESOURCES IMMEDIATELY ACCESSIBLE TO MEET HIS/HER/THEIR NEEDS?		
34. HAVE YOU EXPLAINED TO THE REPATRIATE THAT THE INFORMATION OBTAINED IS PROTECTED UNDER THE PRIVACY ACT AND WILL BE USED SOLELY FOR THE PURPOSE OF ESTABLISHING ELIGIBILITY FOR AND ADMINISTERING THE U.S. REPATRIATION PROGRAM?		
35. HAS THE REPATRIATE SIGNED THE HHS REPAYMENT-LOAN AGREEMENT? *(Agreement must be attached to file.)*		
36. HAS THE REPATRIATE BEEN GIVEN INFORMATION/REFERRAL FOR ASSISTANCE AT THE FINAL DESTINATION?		
37. NAME OF INTERVIEWER *(Last, First, Middle Initial)*	38. TELEPHONE NUMBER *(Include Area Code)*	

DD FORM 2585, DEC 2007   Reset   Page 9 of 10 Pages

Figure F-1. Department of Defense Form 2585, Repatriation Processing Center Processing Sheet (cont.)

SECTION VI - ASSISTANCE PROVIDED DOD PERSONNEL - TO BE COMPLETED BY REPATRIATION PROCESSING CENTER

39. IF NO SERVICES WERE PROVIDED, X THIS BLOCK ⟶		
40. SERVICES PROVIDED *(X as applicable)*	**41. COSTS**	
a. TRANSPORTATION	a. TRANSPORTATION	
b. FINANCIAL *(Advance per diem)*	b. FINANCIAL *(Amount paid)* VOUCHER NUMBER *(for per diem)*	
c. AMERICAN RED CROSS (ARC)	c. AMERICAN RED CROSS (ARC)	
d. HOUSING	42. TOTAL COST	0.00
e. MEDICAL/OTHER		
f. LEGAL SERVICES		
g. CHAPLAIN ASSISTANCE		
h. FAMILY CENTER ASSISTANCE		

SECTION VII - EXIT INFORMATION - TO BE COMPLETED BY REPATRIATION PROCESSING CENTER

43. EXIT FROM PROCESSING CENTER DATE *(YYYYMMDD)*	44. EXIT FROM PROCESSING CENTER TIME *(Military)*	45. DESTINATION *(City, State, Country)*	
46. TRANSPORTATION CARRIER(S)		47.a. ETA AT DESTINATION *(Military Time)*	b. DATE OF ARRIVAL AT DESTINATION *(YYYYMMDD)*

48. ADDITIONAL REMARKS

DD FORM 2585, DEC 2007   Reset   Page 10 of 10 Pages

Figure F-1. Department of Defense Form 2585, Repatriation Processing Center Processing Sheet (cont.)

APPENDIX G
OPERATIONAL RISK AND SAFETY

1. Risk Management

a. **Principles.** Risk management (RM) is the process of identifying, assessing, and controlling risks arising from operational factors and making decisions that balance risk cost with mission benefits. Four rules can be used to guide the JFC's RM process:

(1) Integrate RM into NEO planning.

(2) Accept no unnecessary risks.

(3) Make risk decisions at the proper command level.

(4) Accept risk if benefits outweigh the potential losses.

b. **Process.** There are five steps to the joint RM process as follows:

(1) **Identify the Hazards.** This is begun during planning and continued throughout the NEO. Each operation has both general and unique hazards. Potential hazards for NEOs are discussed below.

(2) **Assess the Hazards.** Each hazard is analyzed to determine the probability of its causing a problem and the severity of the consequences should such a problem occur. This step concludes with a risk assessment that describes the impact of the combined hazards. The result is a statement that quantifies the risk associated with the NEO—extremely high, high, medium, or low.

(3) **Develop Controls.** Leaders at each command level weigh the risks against the benefits. The higher the risk the more likely a decision should be elevated. Ultimately, a commander will have to decide not to take risk in a particular area or establish controls that will mitigate the risk.

(4) **Implement Controls.** The commander then integrates specific controls into plans, orders, SOPs, training, and rehearsals. Knowledge of these controls must extend to each joint force member.

(5) **Supervise and Evaluate.** Finally, leadership at all levels must supervise to ensure compliance with the established controls. They also must reevaluate their effectiveness and make adjustments accordingly.

c. **Operational Environment.** The conditions that prompt a NEO present the joint force with difficult choices during execution. The force mix of combat, combat support, and combat service support depends upon a sound evaluation of the threat. Further, the operational environment likely will be fluid and may change rapidly from permissive to hostile. Operating aircraft, ships, landing craft, and land vehicles under adverse weather conditions is inherently more hazardous. This situation can be exacerbated by the general unfamiliarity of joint force personnel with the operational area.

d. **Potential Hazards.** Hazards may be identified by brainstorming the possibilities within the categories of mission, adversary or enemy, terrain and weather, troops and support available, and time available. The following list contains typical hazards (not an all-inclusive list) that should be considered when planning a NEO.

(1) Accelerated deployment with short planning and preparation time.

(2) Urban terrain—congestion, unfamiliar local customs/laws.

(3) Temperature/humidity extremes.

(4) Underdeveloped infrastructure—roads, ports, aircraft facilities, communications.

(5) Water availability/contamination.

(6) Disease vectors.

(7) Fatigue due to jet lag or 24/7 operations.

(8) HQ/command post facilities and location.

(9) Chain of command clarity.

(10) Local populace interference.

(11) Spontaneous terrorism/insurgency activity.

(12) Night operations.

(13) Rotary-wing operating area characteristics—wires, LZ conditions, density altitude, forward arming and refueling points.

(14) Vehicle operations—speed, loading and unloading noncombatants, overloading, bridge capacities, and escorts.

(15) Weapons/ordnance handling.

(16) Disabled vehicles/aircraft recovery.

(17) PR.

(18) Ship/landing craft operations—slippery spots, tiedowns, flight deck operations, hearing, and head protection.

(19) Evacuation route characteristics—roadblock potential, trafficability, and threat exposure.

(20) Fratricide potential.

e. **Reaction Force.** Because the operational environment can change quickly, a reaction force capable of protecting the NEO force elements and noncombatants from adversary advances is imperative. This force should be on short-notice alert and positioned close to the operating area.

f. **Hazard Awareness.** While joint force members will be informed of the hazards and mitigating controls associated with the military operation, noncombatants likely will be unaware. Further, the general alertness of the noncombatants will be impaired (to some degree) by stress and fatigue resulting from their sudden departure.

2. Safety Considerations

a. **Command Evaluation.** All commanders involved in a NEO are responsible for the safety of their personnel. The JFC and subordinate and supporting commanders share responsibility for the safety of noncombatants with the ambassador. This unique situation requires that the commanders carefully evaluate the associated risks discussed below considering the general unfamiliarity of joint force personnel with the operational area and evacuees unfamiliarity with military procedures and equipment. Thereafter, specific safety precautions should be briefed and implemented to mitigate the operational risks.

b. **Protecting the Force.** Before beginning any NEO, certain standard safety procedures should be implemented as follows:

(1) Brief joint force personnel on the safety aspects and necessary precautions that must be considered for safe operations. When more than one operation takes place in parallel, personnel should be assured that the hazards of any one operation will not inadvertently affect any of the other operations.

(2) Conduct an inspection to determine the physical condition of equipment.

(3) Ensure that personnel who have been instructed and/or given written instructions do, in fact, understand these instructions; ensure that certifications for all operations requiring certified operators are current.

(4) Exercise all equipment.

(5) Ensure that appropriate safety devices are used and worn and that safety procedures are followed.

(6) Brief all personnel on the special safety procedures to be taken when working near noncombatants.

(7) NEOs that involve operations on or near water can be particularly dangerous because of adverse weather, operational task hazards, and adversary action. The efficiency of an operation may also be seriously curtailed by carelessness of personnel who permit dangerous conditions to exist or fail to repair faulty equipment. The following special precautionary steps should be taken to prevent accidents.

(a) **Shipboard Safety.** Accidents aboard ship most frequently result from falls, explosions, falling objects, faulty electrical equipment, unsafe handling procedures, and lack of protection for the eyes and extremities. Life jackets are required during loading, transport, and unloading evolutions with landing craft. Landing craft should be equipped with swimmers qualified in lifesaving techniques. All lines on deck should be made up in such a manner that no one can get tangled in them or trip on them. Rigging must be properly stowed and frequently and properly inspected and maintained. All personnel should wear proper clothing and use correct tools and safety gear.

(b) **Bulk Petroleum Products.** Oil and grease spillage should not be allowed to accumulate on decks; spillage should be wiped up as it occurs. When fuel is being distributed, no bare lights, lighted cigarettes, or any electrical apparatus that have a tendency to spark should be permitted within 50 feet of an oil hose or fuel tank. Only spark-proof tools will be used to connect or disconnect fuel lines.

(c) **Fire Prevention.** "No Smoking" signs will be posted wherever potential fire hazards exist. Smoking will be permitted only in designated areas.

(d) **Embarkation and Debarkation.** Personnel embarkation and debarkation at ships moored offshore should only be conducted in sea state three or below.

(e) **Protective Gear.** Personnel should wear protective headgear and hearing protection. The ship's officers should brief embarked military personnel and noncombatants on any special safety requirements.

c. **Protecting Evacuees.** Although the ambassador is ultimately responsible for the safety of US citizens, the JFC shares that responsibility since the evacuees will be in the custody and direct control of the joint force during the military operation. The following considerations are provided to enhance the protection and safety of evacuees.

(1) **Safety Briefing.** This brief should be part of the reception and search station brief described in Chapter VI, "Evacuee Processing."

(2) **Manning and Expertise.** Adequate manning of the various NEO force elements and stations is key to help evacuees avoid hazardous situations. An adequate presence of embassy and joint force personnel in a supervisory role accompanied by interpreters aids communication with the evacuees, enhancing their awareness of hazardous conditions and overall safety of the various movement and loading evolutions.

d. **Accident Reporting.** Procedures for reporting ground and aviation accidents are well established within Service chains of command. However, the JFC should establish temporary procedures (i.e., accident reporting SOP) that accommodate Service procedures and keep the JFC informed. Typically, there will be an initial telephonic report. Thereafter, a hard-copy report is forwarded up the chain of command. The content of each type of report should be specified in the joint force SOP.

Intentionally Blank

APPENDIX H
REFERENCES

The development of JP 3-68 is based upon the following primary references.

1. General

    a. Executive Order 12656, *Assignment of Emergency Preparedness Responsibilities*, as amended.

    b. Department of State *Emergency Planning Handbook*, 12 FAH-1.

2. Department of Defense

    a. *Memorandum of Agreement Between Departments of State and Defense on the Protection and Evacuation of US Citizens and Nationals and Designated Aliens from Threatened Areas Overseas.*

    b. DODD 2000.11, *Procedures for Handling Requests for Political Asylum and Temporary Refuge.*

    c. DODD 3025.14, *Protection and Evacuation of US Citizens and Designated Aliens in Danger Areas Abroad.*

    d. DODD 5105.75, *Department of Defense Operations at US Embassies.*

    e. DOD Foreign Clearance Guide (www.fcg.pentagon.mil).

    f. *Joint Plan for Department of Defense Noncombatant Repatriation. (Non-Emergency)*, Headquarters, Department of the Army.

3. Chairman of the Joint Chiefs of Staff

    a. *Joint Strategic Capabilities Plan, (JSCP).*

    b. JP 1, *Doctrine for the Armed Forces of the United States.*

    c. JP 1-0, *Personnel Support to Joint Operations.*

    d. JP 2-0, *Joint Intelligence.*

    e. JP 3-0, *Joint Operations.*

    f. JP 3-08, *Interorganizational Coordination During Joint Operations.*

g. JP 3-11, *Operations in Chemical, Biological, Radiological, and Nuclear (CBRN) Environments.*

h. JP 3-13, *Information Operations.*

i. JP 3-13.2, *Military Information Support Operations.*

j. JP 3-17, *Air Mobility Operations.*

k. JP 3-33, *Joint Task Force Headquarters.*

l. JP 3-50, *Personnel Recovery.*

m. JP 3-57, *Civil-Military Operations.*

n. JP 3-61, *Public Affairs.*

o. JP 4-0, *Joint Logistics.*

p. JP 4-02, *Health Service Support.*

q. JP 4-06, *Mortuary Affairs.*

r. JP 6-0, *Joint Communications System.*

s. CJCSI 3121.01B, *Standing Rules of Engagement/Standing Rules for the Use of Force for US Forces.*

t. Chairman of the Joint Chiefs of Staff Manual (CJCSM) 3122.02C, *Joint Operation Planning and Execution System (JOPES), Volume III (Crisis Action Time-Phased Force and Deployment Data Development and Deployment Execution).*

u. CJCSM 3122.03C, *Joint Operation Planning and Execution System, Volume II Planning Formats.*

v. CJCSI 3110.07C, *Guidance Concerning Chemical, Biological, Radiological, and Nuclear Defense and Employment of Riot Control Agents and Herbicides.*

4. Other

a. AJP 3.4.2, *Allied Joint Doctrine for Noncombatant Evacuation Operations.*

b. Field Manual 90-29, *Noncombatant Evacuation Operations.*

c. Center for Naval Analysis 37 39-0003, *Noncombatant Evacuation Operations (NEOs): An Analyst's How-To Guide.*

APPENDIX J
ADMINISTRATIVE INSTRUCTIONS

1. User Comments

Users in the field are highly encouraged to submit comments on this publication to: Commander, United States Joint Forces Command, Joint Warfighting Center, ATTN: Joint Doctrine Group, 116 Lake View Parkway, Suffolk, VA 23435-2697. These comments should address content (accuracy, usefulness, consistency, and organization), writing, and appearance.

2. Authorship

The lead agent for this publication is the US Marine Corps. The Joint Staff doctrine sponsor for this publication is the Director for Operations (J-3).

3. Supersession

This publication supersedes JP 3-68, 22 January 2007, *Noncombatant Evacuation Operations*.

4. Change Recommendations

a. Recommendations for urgent changes to this publication should be submitted:

```
TO:     CG MCCDC QUANTICO VA//C427//
        JOINT STAFF WASHINGTON DC//J3//
        JOINT STAFF WASHINGTON DC//J7-JEDD//
        CDRUSJFCOM SUFFOLK VA//JT10//
```

Routine changes should be submitted electronically to Commander, Joint Warfighting Center, Joint Doctrine Group and info the Lead Agent and the Director for Operational Plans and Joint Force Development J-7/JEDD via the CJCS JEL at http://www.dtic.mil/doctrine.

b. When a Joint Staff directorate submits a proposal to the Chairman of the Joint Chiefs of Staff that would change source document information reflected in this publication, that directorate will include a proposed change to this publication as an enclosure to its proposal. The Services and other organizations are requested to notify the Joint Staff/J-7 when changes to source documents reflected in this publication are initiated.

c. Record of Changes:

CHANGE NUMBER	COPY NUMBER	DATE OF CHANGE	DATE ENTERED	POSTED BY	REMARKS

5. Distribution of Printed Publications

Local reproduction is authorized and access to unclassified publications is unrestricted. However, access to and reproduction authorization for classified joint publications must be in accordance with DOD 5200.1-R, *Information Security Program.*

6. Distribution of Electronic Publications

a. Joint Staff J-7 will not print copies of JPs for distribution. Electronic versions are available at https://jdeis.js.mil (NIPRNET), and https://jdeis.js.smil.mil (SIPRNET) and on the JEL at http://www.dtic.mil/doctrine (NIPRNET).

b. Only approved joint publications and joint test publications are releasable outside the combatant commands, Services, and Joint Staff. Release of any classified joint publication to foreign governments or foreign nationals must be requested through the local embassy (Defense Attaché Office) to DIA Foreign Liaison/IE-3, 200 MacDill Blvd., Bolling AFB, Washington, DC 20340-5100.

GLOSSARY
PART I—ABBREVIATIONS AND ACRONYMS

AE	aeromedical evacuation
AJP	allied joint publication
AMC	Air Mobility Command
AOR	area of responsibility
ARG	amphibious ready group
C2	command and control
CA	civil affairs
CBRN	chemical, biological, radiological, and nuclear
CCDR	combatant commander
CDRUSNORTHCOM	Commander, United States Northern Command
CDRUSPACOM	Commander, United States Pacific Command
CDRUSSOCOM	Commander, United States Special Operations Command
CDRUSSOUTHCOM	Commander, United States Southern Command
CI	counterintelligence
CJCS	Chairman of the Joint Chiefs of Staff
CJCSI	Chairman of the Joint Chiefs of Staff instruction
CJCSM	Chairman of the Joint Chiefs of Staff manual
CJTF	commander, joint task force
CMO	civil-military operations
COA	course of action
COM	chief of mission
CONOPS	concept of operations
CONUS	continental United States
COS	chief of station
DAO	defense attaché office
DATT	defense attaché
DCM	deputy chief of mission
DD	Department of Defense (form)
DHHS	Department of Health and Human Services
DHS	Department of Homeland Security
DJTFAC	deployable joint task force augmentation cell
DMDC	defense manpower data center
DOD	Department of Defense
DODD	Department of Defense directive
DOS	Department of State
DSPD	defense support to public diplomacy
DVD	digital video disc
DZ	drop zone
EAC	emergency action committee
EAP	emergency action plan

ECC	evacuation control center
EOD	explosive ordnance disposal
EPH	emergency planning handbook
EW	electronic warfare
FAH	foreign affairs handbook
FAST	fleet antiterrorism security team
FCE	forward command element
FPD	force protection detachment
GCC	geographic combatant commander
GEOINT	geospatial intelligence
GIBCO	geospatial intelligence base for contingency operations
GPMRC	Global Patient Movement Requirements Center
GSO	general services officer
HLZ	helicopter landing zone
HN	host nation
HNS	host-nation support
HQ	headquarters
HUMINT	human intelligence
IAW	in accordance with
ID	initiating directive
IGO	intergovernmental organization
IMO	information management officer
IO	information operations
ISB	intermediate staging base
JFC	joint force commander
JIOC	joint intelligence operations center
JOA	joint operations area
JPASE	joint public affairs support element
JP	joint publication
JRCC	joint reception coordination center
JSPOC	Joint Space Operations Center
JTF	joint task force
LFA	lead federal agency
LNO	liaison officer
LZ	landing zone
MCSFR	Marine Corps security force regiment
MEDEVAC	medical evacuation
MEU	Marine expeditionary unit
MILDEC	military deception

MISO	military information support operations
MIST	military information support team
MNF	multinational force
MNFC	multinational force commander
MOA	memorandum of agreement
MOU	memorandum of understanding
MSD	mobile security division
MSG	Marine security guard
NATO	North Atlantic Treaty Organization
NEO	noncombatant evacuation operation
NEOCC	noncombatant evacuation operation coordination center
NGA	National Geospatial-Intelligence Agency
NGO	nongovernmental organization
NIST	national intelligence support team
NSG	National System for Geospatial Intelligence
NST	National Geospatial-Intelligence Agency support team
NTS	noncombatant evacuations operation tracking system
OIC	officer in charge
OPCON	operational control
OPLAN	operation plan
OPSEC	operations security
PA	public affairs
PAO	public affairs officer
PCRTS	primary casualty receiving and treatment ship
PM	patient movement
POC	point of contact
PR	personnel recovery
PSO	post security officer
RCA	riot control agent
RLG	regional liaison group
RM	risk management
RMO	regional Marine officer
ROE	rules of engagement
RSO	regional security officer
RST	religious support team
SAO	security assistance officer
SATCOM	satellite communications
SC	strategic communication
SDO	senior defense official
SECAF	Secretary of the Air Force
SECARMY	Secretary of the Army

SecDef	Secretary of Defense
SECNAV	Secretary of the Navy
SECSTATE	Secretary of State
SIPRNET	SECRET Internet Protocol Router Network
SITREP	situation report
SJFHQ(CE)	standing joint force headquarters (core element)
SOF	special operations forces
SOFA	status-of-forces agreement
SOP	standing operating procedure
SROE	standing rules of engagement
TCN	third country national
TPFDD	time-phased force and deployment data
TPMRC	theater patient movement requirements center
UCMJ	Uniform Code of Military Justice
UN	United Nations
USAID	United States Agency for International Development
USCIS	United States Citizenship and Immigration Services
USDAO	United States defense attaché office
USG	United States Government
USSTRATCOM	United States Strategic Command
USTRANSCOM	United States Transportation Command
VIP	very important person
WLG	Washington Liaison Group

aeromedical evacuation. The movement of patients under medical supervision to and between medical treatment facilities by air transportation. Also called **AE.** (JP 1-02. SOURCE: JP 4-02)

all appropriate action. Action taken in self-defense that is reasonable in intensity, duration, and magnitude, based on all the facts known to the commander at the time. (Approved for incorporation into JP 1-02 with JP 3-68 as the source JP.)

authorized departure. A procedure, short of ordered departure, by which mission employees or dependents or both, are permitted to leave post in advance of normal rotation when the national interests or imminent threat to life require it. (JP 1-02. SOURCE: JP 3-68)

Automated Repatriation Reporting System. The Defense Manpower Data Center uses this system to track the status of noncombatant evacuees after they have arrived in an initial safe haven in the United States. (JP 1-02. SOURCE: JP 3-68)

command-sponsored dependent. A dependent entitled to travel to overseas commands at government expense and endorsed by the appropriate military commander to be present in a dependent's status. (Approved for incorporation into JP 1-02.)

counterintelligence. Information gathered and activities conducted to protect against espionage, other intelligence activities, sabotage, or assassinations conducted by or on behalf of foreign governments or elements thereof, foreign organizations, or foreign persons, or international terrorist activities. Also called **CI.** (JP 1-02. SOURCE: JP 2-0)

country team. The senior, in-country, US coordinating and supervising body, headed by the chief of the US diplomatic mission, and composed of the senior member of each represented US department or agency, as desired by the chief of the US diplomatic mission. Also called **CT.** (JP 1-02. SOURCE: JP 3-07.4)

dependents/immediate family. An employee's spouse; children who are unmarried and under age 21 years or who, regardless of age, are physically or mentally incapable of self-support; dependent parents, including step and legally adoptive parents of the employee's spouse; and dependent brothers and sisters, including step and legally adoptive brothers and sisters of the employee's spouse who are unmarried and under 21 years of age or who, regardless of age, are physically or mentally incapable of self-support. (JP 1-02. SOURCE: JP 3-68)

dislocated civilian. A broad term primarily used by the Department of Defense that includes a displaced person, an evacuee, an internally displaced person, a migrant, a refugee, or a stateless person. Also called **DC.** (JP 1-02. SOURCE: JP 3-29)

emergency action committee. An organization established at a foreign service post by the chief of mission or principal officer for the purpose of directing and coordinating the post's response to contingencies. It consists of consular representatives and members of other local US Government agencies in a foreign country who assist in the implementation of a Department of State emergency action plan. Also called **EAC.** (JP 1-02. SOURCE: JP 3-68)

evacuation. 1. Removal of a patient by any of a variety of transport means (air, ground, rail, or sea) from a theater of military operation, or between health service support capabilities, for the purpose of preventing further illness or injury, providing additional care, or providing disposition of patients from the military health care system. (JP 4-02) 2. The clearance of personnel, animals, or materiel from a given locality. (JP 3-68) 3. The controlled process of collecting, classifying, and shipping unserviceable or abandoned materiel, US or foreign, to appropriate reclamation, maintenance, technical intelligence, or disposal facilities. (JP 4-09) 4. The ordered or authorized departure of noncombatants from a specific area by Department of State, Department of Defense, or appropriate military commander. This refers to the movement from one area to another in the same or different countries. The evacuation is caused by unusual or emergency circumstances and applies equally to command or non-command sponsored family members. (JP 3-68) (Approved for incorporation into JP 1-02 with JP 3-68 as the source JP for Definition #2; JP 4-09 as the source JP for Definition #3; and JP 3-68 as the source JP for Definition #4.)

evacuee. A civilian removed from a place of residence by military direction for reasons of personal security or the requirements of the military situation. (JP 1-02. SOURCE: JP 3-57)

force sequencing. The phased introduction of forces into and out of the operational area. (JP 1-02. SOURCE: JP 3-68)

foreign service national. Foreign nationals who provide clerical, administrative, technical, fiscal, and other support at foreign service posts abroad and are not citizens of the United States. The term includes third country nationals who are individuals employed by a United States mission abroad and are neither a citizen of the United States nor of the country to which assigned for duty. Also called **FSN.** (JP 1-02. SOURCE: JP 3-68)

geospatial intelligence base for contingency operations. A mobile visualization tool available through National Geospatial-Intelligence Agency and the Defense Logistics Agency. Applications are broad, including the capability to become familiar with a foreign environment, develop a battle scene, plan and execute noncombatant evacuations, contingency operations, urban area missions, and provide access to geospatial data where networks or infrastructure have been damaged or do not exist. Also called **GIBCO.** (Approved for inclusion in JP 1-02.)

geospatial-intelligence contingency package. None. (Approved for removal from JP 1-02.)

hostile environment. Operational environment in which hostile forces have control as well as the intent and capability to effectively oppose or react to the operations a unit intends to conduct. (JP 1-02. SOURCE: JP 3-0)

host nation. A nation which receives the forces and/or supplies of allied nations and/or NATO organizations to be located on, to operate in, or to transit through its territory. Also called **HN.** (JP 1-02. SOURCE: JP 3-57)

host-nation support. Civil and/or military assistance rendered by a nation to foreign forces within its territory during peacetime, crises or emergencies, or war based on agreements mutually concluded between nations. Also called **HNS.** (JP 1-02. SOURCE: JP 4-0)

intermediate staging base. A tailorable, temporary location used for staging forces, sustainment and/or extraction into and out of an operational area. Also called **ISB.** (JP 1-02. SOURCE: JP 3-35)

joint reception coordination center. The organization, established by the Department of the Army as the designated Department of Defense executive agent for the repatriation of noncombatants, that ensures Department of Defense personnel and noncombatants receive adequate assistance and support for an orderly and expedient debarkation, movement to final destination in the United States, and appropriate follow-on assistance at the final destination. Also called **JRCC.** (JP 1-02. SOURCE: JP 3-68)

joint task force. A joint force that is constituted and so designated by the Secretary of Defense, a combatant commander, a subunified commander, or an existing joint task force commander. Also called **JTF.** (JP 1-02. SOURCE: JP 1)

liaison. That contact or intercommunication maintained between elements of military forces or other agencies to ensure mutual understanding and unity of purpose and action. (JP 1-02. SOURCE: JP 3-08)

military information support operations. Planned operations to convey selected information and indicators to foreign audiences to influence their emotions, motives, objective reasoning, and ultimately the behavior of foreign governments, organizations, groups, and individuals. The purpose of military information support operations is to induce or reinforce foreign attitudes and behavior favorable to the originator's objectives. Also called **MISO.** (JP 1-02. SOURCE: JP 3-13.2)

multinational force. A force composed of military elements of nations who have formed an alliance or coalition for some specific purpose. Also called **MNF.** (JP 1-02. SOURCE: JP 1)

multinational force commander. A general term applied to a commander who exercises command authority over a military force composed of elements from two or more nations. The extent of the multinational force commander's command authority is determined by the participating nations. Also called **MNFC.** (JP 1-02. SOURCE: JP 3-16)

noncombatant evacuation operations. Operations directed by the Department of State or other appropriate authority, in conjunction with the Department of Defense, whereby noncombatants are evacuated from foreign countries when their lives are endangered by war, civil unrest, or natural disaster to safe havens as designated by the Department of State. Also called **NEOs.** (Approved for incorporation into JP 1-02.)

noncombatant evacuation operations tracking system. An automated data processing hardware and software package that has the capability to provide evacuee in-transit visibility to combatant commanders and senior leadership during the conduct of a noncombatant evacuation operation. Also called **NTS.** (Approved for inclusion in JP 1-02.)

noncombatant evacuees. 1. US citizens who may be ordered to evacuate by competent authority include: a. civilian employees of all agencies of the US Government and their dependents, except as noted in 2a below; b. military personnel of the Armed Forces of the United States specifically designated for evacuation as noncombatants; and c. dependents of members of the Armed Forces of the United States. 2. US (and non-US) citizens who may be authorized or assisted (but not necessarily ordered to evacuate) by competent authority include: a. civilian employees of US Government agencies and their dependents, who are residents in the country concerned on their own volition, but express the willingness to be evacuated; b. private US citizens and their dependents; c. military personnel and dependents of members of the Armed Forces of the United States outlined in 1c above, short of an ordered evacuation; and d. designated personnel, including dependents of persons listed in 1a through 1c above, as prescribed by the Department of State. (JP 1-02. SOURCE: JP 3-68)

ordered departure. A procedure by which the number of US Government personnel, their dependents, or both are reduced at a foreign service post. Departure is directed by the Department of State (initiated by the chief of mission or the Secretary of State) to designated safe havens with implementation of the combatant commander noncombatant evacuation operations plan. (JP 1-02. SOURCE: JP 3-68)

permissive environment. Operational environment in which host country military and law enforcement agencies have control as well as the intent and capability to assist operations that a unit intends to conduct. (JP 1-02. SOURCE: JP 3-0)

personnel recovery. The sum of military, diplomatic, and civil efforts to prepare for and execute the recovery and reintegration of isolated personnel. Also called **PR.** (JP 1-02. SOURCE: JP 3-50)

procedures. Standard, detailed steps that prescribe how to perform specific tasks. (JP 1-02. SOURCE: CJCSI 5120.02)

public affairs. Those public information, command information, and community engagement activities directed toward both the external and internal publics with interest in the Department of Defense. Also called **PA.** (JP 1-02. SOURCE: JP 3-61)

regional liaison group. A combined Department of State–Department of Defense element collocated with a combatant command for the purpose of coordinating post emergency evacuation plans. Also called **RLG.** (JP 1-02. SOURCE: JP 3-68)

repatriation. 1. The procedure whereby American citizens and their families are officially processed back into the United States subsequent to an evacuation. (JP 3-68). 2. The release and return of enemy prisoners of war to their own country in accordance with the 1949 Geneva Convention Relative to the Treatment of Prisoners of War. (JP 1-0). (Approved for incorporation into JP 1-02 with JP 3-68 as the source JP for Definition #1.)

risk management. The process of identifying, assessing, and controlling risks arising from operational factors and making decisions that balance risk cost with mission benefits. Also called **RM.** (JP 1-02. SOURCE: JP 2-0)

rules of engagement. Directives issued by competent military authority that delineate the circumstances and limitations under which United States forces will initiate and/or continue combat engagement with other forces encountered. Also called **ROE.** (JP 1-02. SOURCE: JP 1-04)

safe haven. 1. Designated area(s) to which noncombatants of the United States Government's responsibility and commercial vehicles and materiel may be evacuated during a domestic or other valid emergency. (JP 3-68) 2. Temporary storage provided to Department of Energy classified shipment transporters at Department of Defense facilities in order to assure safety and security of nuclear material and/or nonnuclear classified material. Also includes parking for commercial vehicles containing Class A or Class B explosives. (JP 4-01.6) 3. A protected body of water or the well deck of an amphibious ship used by small craft operating offshore for refuge from storms or heavy seas. (JP 4-01.6) (Approved for incorporation into JP 1-02 with JP 3-68 as the source JP for Definition #1.)

tactics. The employment and ordered arrangement of forces in relation to each other. (JP 1-02. SOURCE: CJCSI 5120.02)

techniques. Non-prescriptive ways or methods used to perform missions, functions, or tasks. (JP 1-02. SOURCE: CJCSI 5120.02)

uncertain environment. Operational environment in which host government forces, whether opposed to or receptive to operations that a unit intends to conduct, do not have totally effective control of the territory and population in the intended operational area. (JP 1-02. SOURCE: JP 3-0)

warden system. An informal method of communication used to pass information to US citizens during emergencies. (JP 1-02. SOURCE: JP 3-68)

Washington Liaison Group. An interagency committee and/or joint monitoring body, chaired by the Department of State with representation from the Department of Defense, established to coordinate the preparation and implementation of plans for evacuation of United States citizens abroad in emergencies. Also called **WLG.** (JP 1-02. SOURCE: JP 3-68)

JOINT DOCTRINE PUBLICATIONS HIERARCHY

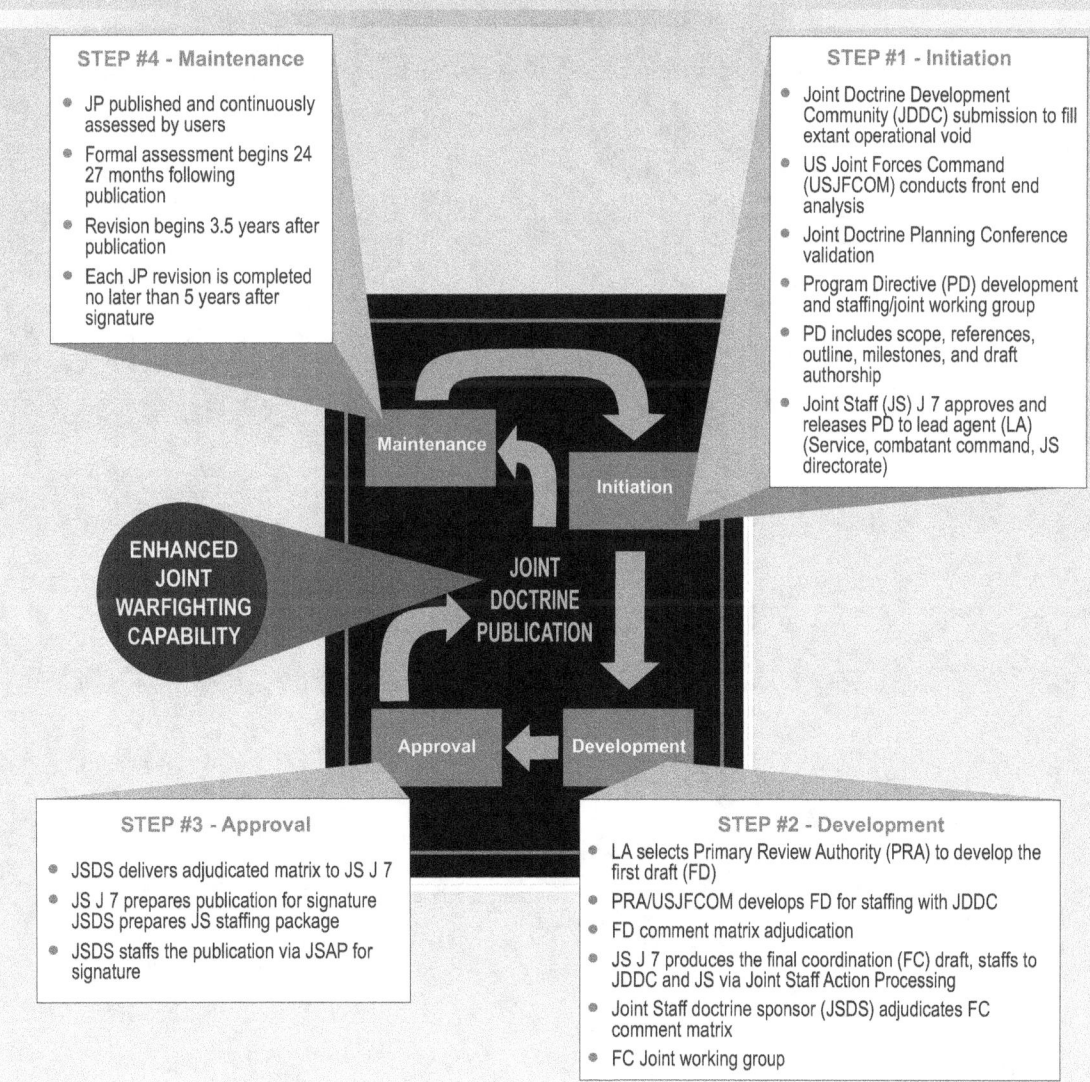

JP 1
JOINT DOCTRINE

JP 1-0	JP 2-0	JP 3-0	JP 4-0	JP 5-0	JP 6-0
PERSONNEL	INTELLIGENCE	OPERATIONS	LOGISTICS	PLANS	COMMUNICATIONS SYSTEMS

All joint publications are organized into a comprehensive hierarchy as shown in the chart above. **Joint Publication (JP) 3-68** is in the **Operations** series of joint doctrine publications. The diagram below illustrates an overview of the development process:

STEP #4 - Maintenance

- JP published and continuously assessed by users
- Formal assessment begins 24 27 months following publication
- Revision begins 3.5 years after publication
- Each JP revision is completed no later than 5 years after signature

STEP #1 - Initiation

- Joint Doctrine Development Community (JDDC) submission to fill extant operational void
- US Joint Forces Command (USJFCOM) conducts front end analysis
- Joint Doctrine Planning Conference validation
- Program Directive (PD) development and staffing/joint working group
- PD includes scope, references, outline, milestones, and draft authorship
- Joint Staff (JS) J 7 approves and releases PD to lead agent (LA) (Service, combatant command, JS directorate)

ENHANCED JOINT WARFIGHTING CAPABILITY

Maintenance

Initiation

JOINT DOCTRINE PUBLICATION

Approval

Development

STEP #3 - Approval

- JSDS delivers adjudicated matrix to JS J 7
- JS J 7 prepares publication for signature JSDS prepares JS staffing package
- JSDS staffs the publication via JSAP for signature

STEP #2 - Development

- LA selects Primary Review Authority (PRA) to develop the first draft (FD)
- PRA/USJFCOM develops FD for staffing with JDDC
- FD comment matrix adjudication
- JS J 7 produces the final coordination (FC) draft, staffs to JDDC and JS via Joint Staff Action Processing
- Joint Staff doctrine sponsor (JSDS) adjudicates FC comment matrix
- FC Joint working group